FORGIVENESS AND RECONCILIATION

Retreat Leader Guide
WORKBOOK
RICHARD T. CASE

To my wife, Linda, who has learned these great truths of forgiveness and then demonstrated them to me and all our family and friends in real life. She understands that forgiveness is critical to live a life of freedom; that she can get there 100 percent of the time—all the time; and that this is a gift of God and a heart issue between her and God—a separate issue from reconciliation. With forgiveness, she then has learned the truths of reconciliation—that this requires two parties dealing with truth together; and that if the other party is not willing to go to truth, she can live with not being reconciled—still living in forgiveness and freedom. She is a continual reminder of how this important element of life (perhaps one of the most important since we live in a world where people, even those close to us, will continually hurt and offend us) is to be received and experienced so we are never burdened or oppressed. She always lives in joy, and thus brings true joy to me as we walk with God together. A honor to experience this together, honey!

Acknowledgments

We wish to thank all of the leaders of our **Ministry: Living Waters—ABIDE Ministries!** These leaders daily and faithfully also have learned to receive and live out forgiveness/reconciliation—and together are always giving this away to others who are being called by God to receive release and freedom in this most critical area of life. Thank you all:

These leaders are:

Jake & Mary Beckel
Joe & Leigh Bogar
Rich & Janet Cocchiaro
Larry & Sherry Collet
David & Melissa Dunkel
Tom & Susanne Ewing
Rick & Kelly Ferris
Joel & Christina Gunn
Scott & Terry Hitchcock
Chris & Jaclyn Hoover
Rick & Nancy Hoover
Tad & Monica Jones
Ed & Becky Kobel
Don & Rachelle Light
Chris & Heidi May
Terry & Josephine Noetzel
Steve & Carolyn Van Ooteghem
Preston & Lynda Pitts
Dan & Kathy Rocconi
Bob & Keri Rockwell
John & Michelle Santaferraro
Allyson & Denny Weinberg
Neal & Kathy Weisenburger

FORGIVENESS AND RECONCILIATION
PUBLISHED BY LIVING WATERS—ABIDE MINISTRIES
7615 Lemon Gulch Way
Castle Rock, CO 80108

Unless otherwise noted, all Scripture quotations are from the ESV® Bible (The Holy Bible, English Standard Version®), copyright © 2001 by Crossway Bibles, a publishing ministry of Good News Publishers. Used by permission. All rights reserved.

ISBN: 978-1-7334151-8-7
Copyright © 2024 by Richard T. Case.

All rights reserved. No part of this publication may be reproduced, distributed or transmitted in any form or by any means, including photocopying, recording, or other electronic or mechanical methods, without the prior written permission of the publisher.

Publisher's Cataloging-in-Publication data

Names:
Title:
Description: .
Identifiers: ISBN | LCCN
Subjects:

Printed in the United States of America 2024 — 1st ed

TABLE OF CONTENTS

Introduction 1

Lesson One:
What Is Un-Forgiveness? What Contributes To It? 4

Lesson Two:
Why We Withhold Forgiveness? 32

Lesson Three:
What Is Forgiveness? (Part 1)? 40

Lesson Four:
What Is Forgiveness? (Part 2)? 56

Lesson Five:
What Is Reconciliation? (Part 1)? 76

Lesson Six:
What Is Reconciliation? (Part 2)? 104

Lesson Seven:
Ambassadors in Reconciliation 124

Lesson Eight:
Practical Ways of Reconciliation in a Variety of Situations 146

FOREGIVENESS AND RECONCILIATION

INTRODUCTION

INTRODUCTION

The lack of forgiveness and reconciliation within relationships is an issue nearly all people experience. My wife, Linda, and I have been conducting marriage retreats for the past 12 years. In each retreat, almost all of the couples are dealing with these very issues: forgiveness and reconciliation. Lack of forgiveness oftentimes becomes a standard or learned behavior between the husband and wife. But from there, the behavior will spill over into relationships with parents, siblings, children, friends, workers, bosses, etc. Why is this such a problem? Because a lack of forgiveness leads to further negativity. It is true that we all are surrounded by selfish people who hurt and manipulate us to merely obtain what they want, especially what they want us to do for them. As we experience such wounds, frustrations, and opposition, we naturally become angry and then proceed to struggle with what to do with the anger. That anger quickly begins hardening hearts and dissolving intimacy within relationships. We maintain our un-forgiveness because the other party has not admitted or confessed their wrongdoing to us, and therefore, we wait upon them to make things right. Since most people do not respond to wounds by resolving what they have done to us (and often lack the admission of what we have done to them) everyone continues operating in un-forgiveness.

> "The problem with this un-forgiveness is that we are hurting only ourselves—our own soul—and the ability to enjoy our own life."

The problem with this un-forgiveness is that we are hurting only ourselves—our own soul—and the ability to enjoy our own life. Over the years Linda and I have worked to bring healing to people's lives through the power of forgiveness. What has become clear to us in this ministry, however, is that there is great confusion between forgiveness and reconciliation. This course serves to explore the depths of these differences, offer Biblical truths that allow us to live in forgiveness, and then offer reconciliation to those around us. We also will describe how to maintain forgiveness when those around us are unwilling to reconcile.

Case in point: At one of our retreats, a woman expressed deep bitterness toward her father who first had oppressed her as a child and then rejected her as an adult. In fact, he had rejected the entire family after divorcing her mother. Like her, all of her siblings were estranged from their father. During the retreat, the woman processed God's call to forgiveness and offer of reconciliation. She worked through the Word of God until she received that which she so eagerly sought: forgiveness toward her father. Having

INTRODUCTION

experienced the release of forgiving her father, she wanted to share it with the rest of her family. She called each of her siblings and expressed to them the freedom she had so beautifully received. She even went further suggesting that each sibling work through the same process until they, too, fully embraced and received the same forgiveness God was calling them to accept and to extend. Sadly, though, all of her siblings declined and chose to remain enslaved to their bitterness. What her siblings couldn't see was that by choosing bitterness and refusing to forgive actually placed each of them in bondage. As we will see throughout this course, refusing to process un-forgiveness causes continued—but avoidable—pain and angst.

But her story didn't end there. After this precious lady had received forgiveness regarding her father, she then contacted him to offer reconciliation. Her father was pleased to hear from her and was willing to meet. Though he was not able to process much of her actual pain, they did reconcile at a surface level and each experienced and felt the freedom of having regained a lost relationship. Then, less than a week later, her father passed away. This dear lady praised God for the gift of truth and revelation of forgiveness, but also that she was given the opportunity and power to express her love toward her father before he died. Her siblings, on the other hand, chose not to face their bitterness and even added to it by becoming annoyed with the sister who worked to mend the relationship with the father. They continue to be burdened by the bitterness they have developed over the years and now that bitterness cannot be let go. Again, this course will show how we each can come to, receive, and welcome forgiveness regarding those who have hurt us, even when those who have hurt us have passed away, and there is no chance for reconciliation.

This woman's story is, unfortunately, not unique. Most of us have similar stories in our own lives and are living within various levels of un-forgiveness and some level of bitterness. As we will discover, the truth and revelation of God found in the Scriptures declares God's call to us: a call to forgive and to forgive 100 percent of the time. In the same way, God desires that each of us lives in utter and complete freedom, freedom that can only be obtained through forgiveness.

We also will earn that forgiveness does not equal reconciliation, because reconciliation takes two willing parties. While this may feel like a complicated endeavor, we eventually will come to understand the simplicity of our position in the reconciliation process—which always starts and ends with forgiveness.

LESSON 1:
WHAT IS UN-FORGIVENESS? WHAT CONTRIBUTES TO IT?

Why do you think the lack of forgiveness and reconciliation is so prevalent in our day?

How would you define the following?

Forgiveness:
_____
_____
_____
_____
_____
_____
_____
_____

Reconciliation:
_____
_____
_____
_____
_____
_____
_____
_____

How and why do we confuse the two?
_____
_____
_____
_____
_____
_____
_____
_____
_____

> "Where there is no forgiveness, there is no trace of anything resembling a forgiven life, a forgiven person, the evidence of forgiveness, or the evidence of Christ."

LESSON 1:
WHAT IS UN-FORGIVENESS? WHAT CONTRIBUTES TO IT?

We will spend time in this study exploring "forgiveness and reconciliation," both of which impact every life and thus our true enjoyment of life. In these sessions, we will uncover:

1. What "un-forgiveness" is and what contributes to it.

2. Why we withhold forgiveness.

3. What forgiveness is.

4. What reconciliation is.

5. Practical ways of obtaining reconciliation in a variety of situations.

> **Define Un-forgiveness from the following verses:**
> **Read Romans 11:30-32.**
>
> [30] For just as you were at one time disobedient to God but now have received mercy because of their disobedience, [31] so they too have now been disobedient in order that by the mercy shown to you they also may now[a] receive mercy. [32] For God has consigned all to disobedience, that he may have mercy on all.

_____
_____
_____
_____
_____

Forgiveness means that you no longer feel angry or resentful toward someone who has hurt you either through a mistake or offense. Un-forgiveness, simply put, is the absence of forgiveness. By withholding forgiveness, a person allows chaos and evil character traits to run amok. Where there is no forgiveness, there is no trace of anything resembling a forgiven life, a forgiven person, the evidence of forgiveness, or the evidence of Christ.

There can be nothing resembling Christ when our days emphasize bitterness, wrath, and even slander. Each one deeply grieves the heart of a holy God, and since we serve a triune God, such actions also grieve the Holy Spirit. We are called

LESSON 1:
WHAT IS UN-FORGIVENESS? WHAT CONTRIBUTES TO IT?

to abhor such actions and instead embrace those attributes that reflect God Himself: tenderness, mercy, kindness. We are to do these things out of a grateful heart, forgiving others because we have been forgiven.

Of course, we do live in an evil world, full of people who do evil things, and God has given them up to be ruled by their own corrupted minds. Because of this, we must constantly be on guard against those corrupted minds that cannot do anything else but hate their Creator, stir up strife, cultivate deception, and heartily approve of anyone else who does so. Those who walk according to the flesh and those who walk in the Spirit are completely and utterly different, opposite. Those who love God are robed with His righteousness, and their hearts overflow with mercy, humbleness, and truth. It would be naïve to say that Christians never participate in those evils mentioned in Galatians, so it is curious why those who have the Spirit of the living and loving God residing within them, would act so contrarily. One of the reasons for this is simply that they do not forgive. Un-forgiveness is what lies at the roots of bitterness, wrath, anger, slander. When our hearts are wounded by circumstances or people who cut to the quick of our hearts or manipulate us, sometimes we choose to hold on to the anger and refuse to forgive them. We remain in the pool of anger and animosity and act out accordingly. For some reason, we have chosen to hold on to our wounds, the bitterness, and our hurt in lieu of forgiving and moving on.

What we are unaware of is that the action of withholding forgiveness imprisons our hearts and souls. It keeps us from living by the Spirit and, in turn, keeps us enslaved to anger, which consequently leads to bitterness. The longer we withhold forgiveness, the more difficult it becomes to offer love, mercy, and kindness to others, or to receive it ourselves. Making a conscious decision to not to get angry isn't enough and doesn't work. We are unable in our own power to resolve our anger and naturally make our way toward forgiveness. Unfortunately for us, the process of anger leading to un-forgiveness happens automatically. We cannot escape its natural progression. Read the following Scriptures:

Is this a choice? Why or why not?

Read Ephesians 4:26-27.

²⁶ Be angry and do not sin; do not let the sun go down on your anger, ²⁷ and give no opportunity to the devil.

LESSON 1:
WHAT IS UN-FORGIVENESS? WHAT CONTRIBUTES TO IT?

_____
_____
_____
_____
_____

> **Read Isaiah 28:16-17.**
>
> [16] therefore thus says the Lord God,
> "Behold, I am the one who has laid[a] as a foundation in Zion,
>   a stone, a tested stone,
> a precious cornerstone, of a sure foundation:
>   'Whoever believes will not be in haste.'
> [17] And I will make justice the line,
>   and righteousness the plumb line;
> and hail will sweep away the refuge of lies,
>   and waters will overwhelm the shelter."

_____
_____
_____
_____
_____

We should start out by being encouraged here. Scripture clearly states that it is okay and perfectly acceptable to be angry. Anger is a natural and God-given emotion. In fact, God himself experiences anger! We were given this natural emotion so that our sense of right and wrong, reality and truth, and our everyday lives collide in a beautiful symphony. However, there is a line drawn in the sand—you can be angry, but do not let the anger cause you to sin. How is this possible? Check all unresolved anger. If we let our anger, our hurt, our betrayal fester, we give the enemy an opportunity to affect us, affect our lives, and affect our relationships with both God and others. We cannot prevent getting angry because we cannot prevent the circumstances that cause anger in the first place, but we need to know our response to such instances can lead to sin. Sin, simply

LESSON 1:
WHAT IS UN-FORGIVENESS? WHAT CONTRIBUTES TO IT?

explained, is to miss the mark. It's an archery term. If you have ever watched an archery event, or even attempted it, you know the archer is always aiming for the center of their target. This is their mark. When they hit it, everyone cheers, and they feel a great sense of accomplishment. But, when they miss their mark, the miss is called a sin. It is the same way in our spiritual lives. We miss our mark each and every time we maintain our anger and continue down the treacherous path to un-forgiveness instead of processing through our hurt so that we reach forgiveness. It is this very unwillingness to forgive that allows the devil a foothold in our lives, causing wounds to deepen into hardness of heart, bitterness, wrath, etc.

But do not stop here, look further. The cornerstone of our faith is Jesus. This cornerstone is unique and is the foundation of true faith. This stone has been created by the tools of justice and righteousness and thus made perfect. So, we know that God acts and reacts justly and operates within righteousness when it comes to our wounds. Justice is, and always has been, God's measuring line, the mark for which He is aiming. So, if justice is God's mark and we have God's Spirit indwelling us, it is natural for us to react with anger to unfairness, wrongdoing, and inequality. Again, this anger is sanctioned by God and has been established as His measuring line automatically dictating our responses. Take a moment to sit back and think about the anger in your own life. What are you angry about? At whom are you angry? What did they do to you? What did they deny you? At what injustices in the world are you infuriated? Take a good introspective account of your own heart and the hurts that have resulted in anger. Write them down if you need to, and then look at the results of the conflicts. You will rightly notice that your response to being angry differs with each circumstance, and that the relationships are strained at differing levels. Remember, our goal, and yours, too, we hope, is not to continue with the way things are. It is to apply the healing balm of forgiveness to each and every circumstance to not only release the bitterness and anger, but also to allow the fullness of Christ's work to have its complete power in you.

Process through the following until you receive clarity and understanding:

We encounter circumstances or people causing injustice every day. The anger and frustration that accompany each event is unique to the people associated with it and to the offense. In our experience, we have noticed that there are basically three differing levels at which humanity typically responds to wounds. These are: Minimal, Partial, and Complete. Let's take a look at each one.

> "The cornerstone of our faith is Jesus. This cornerstone is unique and is the foundation of true faith. This stone has been created by the tools of justice and righteousness and thus made perfect."

LESSON 1:
WHAT IS UN-FORGIVENESS? WHAT CONTRIBUTES TO IT?

1. **Minimal:** not withdrawn or harsh, can talk to the other person, can be in same room, but upset at some level. There is a strain in the relationship; it tends to be short, edgy, somewhat distant; sometimes dogmatic; different.

   You have been wounded. Things like this happen nearly every day, but at the minimal level, you can be upset and even notice a strain on the relationship but not much more. You do not withdraw from your offender or from the hurt experienced and do not act harshly toward them. You are still able to politely talk with them and even be in the same room. Yet, when you do converse, the dialogue tends to be rather short and curt with a slight edge to it. The distance between the two of you can be sensed, and the two of you may act differently or dogmatically toward each other. For instance, let's say you have a lunch date with a friend, but they were a no-show with no warning or explanation. When you email the friend later that day to find out what happened, they simply respond with, "I just got too busy, sorry." Your immediate response is to get a bit miffed that they didn't show enough common courtesy to at least call or text message to cancel. Even though this is a minimal response to the conflict, you still wrestle with the fact that they don't consider not showing up as being disrespectful to you or your friendship. You may not be holding a grudge, but the relationship still feels slightly strained, something that had not been the case previously. As a result of your minimal withdrawal, your friend who cancelled further withdraws in response, and the strain continues to be felt, and potentially deepens if left unresolved or ignored.

2. **Partial:** are separated today. Do not want to talk about it right now. Are mad. Do not want to deal with this person so separate, even if for while, because we have to be together later; is affecting my ability to relate to on a friendly, rationale level. Tend to stuff things further, not resolve, eventually develops roots of bitterness; but later, maybe even tomorrow, act as if things are fine. The relationship is somewhat strained and certainly different; but a new normal is established.

   You have been wounded, this time it is a different circumstance, and there has been an initial separation between you and the one who hurt you. Typically, your reaction would be not to talk about or deal with the issue at hand and act clearly and noticeably angry. At this level, you want nothing to do with your offender, even if you know you must interact with them at a later date. The conflict clearly affects your ability to relate to them on a friendly and/or even rational level. Many times, you may suppress your feelings, which only harms the relationship further instead of resolving the issue at hand. Your relationship is obviously strained, and

LESSON 1:
WHAT IS UN-FORGIVENESS? WHAT CONTRIBUTES TO IT?

the two of you interact with great indifference, but this indifference and strained relationship becomes the new normal for you. Here is a possible scenario to clarify: You are an active member of your church and currently serve on a committee. Another person on the same committee complains to a third party that you are not pulling your weight and often have poor ideas. When you finally hear about what has been said, you become angry and defensive but don't want to confront your opponent. So, what do you do? You find excuses not to show up to the committee meetings (to avoid seeing them) and when you do see them, there is an overwhelming indifference tainted with loathing toward them. Even when he/she speaks, you fail to join in any of the discussions, making sure your silence is noticed and felt. It would be obvious to others, not to mention between the two of you directly, that the relationship is seriously strained, but neither of you wish to resolve the conflict. In response to the issue as a whole, your anxiety increases greatly whenever you think of going to a committee meeting, and you no longer enjoy participating with any of the work done through the group. The conflict has lost you a friend and the joy associated with working with your church.

3. **Complete:** want nothing to do with this person now; cut off all communications. Are mad, and unless the other party apologizes, admits what they did was wrong, how they were hurtful, and works to correct the problem, you are not budging.

Yet again, you are hurt, and this stage is by far the most severe. You want no contact—absolutely nothing to do with the one who harmed you. All communication between the two of you has ceased. You are clearly and noticeably mad and have resolutely decided that unless your offender apologizes and admits they were wrong, reconciliation will not happen. At this stage, nothing will make you change your mind. Example: You and a Christian friend got into a heated argument that resulted in them walking out and slamming the door in your face. Your friend has neither called to discuss the issue nor to discuss anything, for that matter. In response, you refuse to communicate, too. Since you are completely convinced they are the one who owes you an apology, the relationship is broken and any association with them personally (whether through church or work) is ardently avoided.

Do you remember when it was suggested for you to take an account of the anger in your own life? Revisit those circumstances. Before we progress any further, please be willing to go deeper. Has there been anyone in your life you have cut off communication with entirely? Who was it? What caused the separation? Be willing to admit your own contribution to the situation. Is there anyone with whom you used to be friends? What happened to make you now indifferent toward

LESSON 1:
WHAT IS UN-FORGIVENESS? WHAT CONTRIBUTES TO IT?

each other? Can you even remember? Please spend some time praying with the Father to reveal to you more areas in your past and present that need His healing touch of forgiveness. Will it hurt to revisit painful times? Yes, but it is worth every tear you shed if it leads to true and complete healing. Do not be afraid or too stubborn to look at the darkest recesses of your heart. Those doors you refuse to open to others, fling those wide open to Jesus. Allow Him full access to your heart and mind, and He will be faithful to not only reveal the places, memories, and circumstances He wants to heal, He WILL heal them if you let Him.

If you are like most people, you probably have an incredibly long list of harmful actions done and words said to you through the years. Unfortunately, this is not uncommon in today's world, but with the litany of wounds we experience, what necessitates the level at which we respond? Everything has to do with your wound: how it happened, by whom it happened, etc. The events that surround your hurt, everything about its environment, contribute to how we respond.

The level of the response is determined by:

1. **Severity of hurt:**

   If a wound or frustration occurs, and it is temporal or nominal in nature, a minimal response will typically ensue. For example, you are at a restaurant and the waitress is not as attentive as you would like (you have needed a refill for 10 minutes, you are still waiting for some utensils, etc.) or messes up your order (you ordered the grilled chicken with broccoli and received fried chicken with fries). So, you naturally respond in anger. However, because you know the interaction is merely temporary and have no real relationship with the waitress, your response is usually minimal. In the grand scheme of life, this interaction matters little, and you will not have an ongoing level of un-forgiveness. On the other hand, if your mother calls incessantly, making you feel guilty for not visiting enough, the severity of your wound may be quite strong. Why the difference? Two reasons: 1. You have a deep and ongoing relationship with your mother, and 2. the actions are continually being experienced. In this case, your response more than likely will move to the partial or complete level depending on the harshness experienced. This and the next item—frequency of hurt—were what contributed to the partial and then the complete break in the relationship with my mother. It was personal: The words were very severe, and it happened over and over again. Therefore, it became increasingly difficult to let any jab or snide remark go unnoticed or ignored. As a result, my response shifted from partial strain (avoiding being together as much as possible) to complete strain (withdrawing completely and avoiding all contact).

> "Do not be afraid or too stubborn to look at the darkest recesses of your heart. Those doors you refuse to open to others, fling those wide open to Jesus."

LESSON 1:
WHAT IS UN-FORGIVENESS? WHAT CONTRIBUTES TO IT?

2. **Frequency of hurt:**

   If you are wounded once, if it is a single event, your response tends to be minimal (i.e., you are not given credit for all of your contribution in a collaborative work presentation, but it had never happened before). However, if the wound happens repetitively, your response will move to a partial and/or complete one. Let's say that every time you visit with relatives, they make attacking comments about the way you are managing your children or the dating choices you make; and because these remarks are hurtful and not helpful in any way, you have politely asked them to please stop making these comments. However, if your relatives repeatedly ignore your request and continue to make the same comments, the frequency of the offense will increase your level of response.

3. **Current level of frustration about other things:**

   - Tired, weary
   - Worried, anxious
   - Fear
   - Roots of bitterness, anger
   - Grief, sadness
   - Disappointments, resignation

   It is this area in particular that typically leads someone to further disappointment in life, steering them directly toward withholding forgiveness. Your response to all frustrating circumstances can be triggered, or your responses intensified, by your own emotional state as it relates to other areas in your life:

   Tired, weary: If you are worn out, you will find that you tend to be more sensitive; that your emotions are more easily accessed and thus can quickly shift anger to un-forgiveness even with normally trifling circumstances.

   Worried, anxious: If you are experiencing worry and anxiety about things, opposition intensifies these emotions and will, again, quickly trigger deeper levels of un-forgiveness.

   Fear: If you live in general fear or are afraid of future outcomes, there is a strong desire to protect the "safety" of your heart from further negative harm as these can then quickly trigger the deeper emotions that will maintain un-forgiveness.

LESSON 1:
WHAT IS UN-FORGIVENESS? WHAT CONTRIBUTES TO IT?

Roots of bitterness, anger: Your current level of anger and/or bitterness will only serve to intensify new wounds and opposition. Other circumstances will be seen as more frustration and further create injustice in a wounded person's life.

Grief, sadness: If you are experiencing grief due to loss or disappointing events, new hurtful experiences in your life can lead you to experience deeper levels of grief, which then lead to un-forgiveness.

Disappointments, resignation: If you have tried to overcome obstacles in your life in order to deal with those hurting you, you can live in a perpetual state of disappointment or resignation.

All of these, alone or together, can intensify our responses to any hurtful circumstance. Linda and I have found that this is a great scheme the enemy uses: Various terse conditions create strained relationships that intensify our un-forgiveness. Let's take a very practical and real example: If I come home from work tired and weary plus being anxious and disappointed about things not going well at work, it is easy for me to overreact when Linda didn't do something I asked her to do. Uncharacteristically, I snap at her, which leads to her snapping back since my overreaction was out of line. Thus begins the edginess and a very slippery slope toward un-forgiveness. Before we had learned the importance of forgiveness and reconciliation, we would not have dealt with this type of situation at all, much less in a constructive manner. The result of not dealing with situations such as this was each of us carrying around low levels of anger, which would then erupt inappropriately and unexpectedly in various scenarios. Consequently, roots of bitterness developed toward each other, causing the relationship to become more and more strained. When either I failed to fulfill her desires or she failed mine, eruptions in anger became commonplace, and the intensity of the strain in our relationship progressively deepened. Normal situations most people typically overlook became sources of irritation, frustration, and continued overreaction.

4. **Hardness, stubbornness of person hurting me:**

The way in which you react is directly dictated by the way your offender acts toward you. If the one who has hurt you acts harshly and in a very difficult manner, your response level increases. If your offender is stubborn and not willing to process the hurtful action with you, your response level tends to increase. If the one hurting you continues operating in their pride and self-centeredness, then your response tends to immediately lean more toward a partial or complete separation. This was a

LESSON 1:
WHAT IS UN-FORGIVENESS? WHAT CONTRIBUTES TO IT?

big contributor to my anger and un-forgiveness toward my mother. Throughout my life she had had an extremely harsh and stubborn way about her. We were told, in no uncertain terms, that it was either her way or the highway. So, even when she did have legitimate things to challenge me on, my defenses were already permanently up because of the regular verbal battles and power plays I experienced with and by her. To this very day, though I live in forgiveness and freedom, when someone harshly confronts me, I initially have a negative reaction because I faced similarly harsh treatment from my mother.

5. **Emotional escalation of the moment:**

Your own emotions can escalate in the moment and within the conflict depending on which emotions are triggered and in how you are being treated. For example:

- **Words spoken that accuse; attack my character:**

If the wounded party is falsely or harshly accused, such an attack of their character would only deepen their response. In the heat of arguments, it is easy for us to use words that hurt and wound others. We often say things that accuse others within their character, which result in unnecessary wounds. In our early years of marriage, Linda and I frequently used such words as "you always" and "you never" when we argued. These words, spawned from our anger and falsely flung at each other, directly attacked the other's character and were only used to try and win the battle. By using these kinds of words and allowing the roots of bitterness and un-forgiveness to deepen, it became easier and easier to use character assassination the next time around, just to hurt the other person, to harm a beloved spouse.

- **Circumstances that appear to deepen my hurt and anger—whether imagined or real:**

Such circumstances could either be imagined or real. If someone believes that the people opposing them are doing it purposely or callously, whether real or perceived, it can deepen their response to the conflict. This is another great trick of the enemy. We often see this as well during our retreats. The husband in one couple stated inadvertently within the group that he was looking to start a new business. As it turns out, this was news to the wife! With the bombshell given at the retreat, she had assumed her husband had already decided to quit his job and start a new business without even talking to or discussing it with her. As a result, she withdrew from her husband, and Linda and I could clearly see on the

LESSON 1:
WHAT IS UN-FORGIVENESS? WHAT CONTRIBUTES TO IT?

> "A comment or a supposed circumstance can be interpreted in many ways, and if its interpretation causes fear, anxiety, or worry, then it can easily go to anger and frustration."

second day of the retreat their relationship was strained. We called them together and helped them process and verbalize what each was feeling. When the wife stated she was fearful her husband was starting a new business, the husband responded that it was just a fleeting thought, and he hadn't even given it any serious consideration at all! The wife's initial reaction was a false perception, but to her it was real. A comment or a supposed circumstance can be interpreted in many ways, and if its interpretation causes fear, anxiety, or worry, then it can easily go to anger and frustration. This is why it is so critical to continually communicate and make sure there is full understanding and agreement on what is being stated and not to let any circumstance or inadvertent comments throw off our relationships.

Go back to your list of wounds, anger, and broken relationships. This time, take each situation and honestly assess if there were extenuating circumstances that elevated your response. Had you been up all night with a sick child? Did your spouse just get diagnosed with cancer? Was your character being attacked? Were you being yelled at or belittled? Was it the 49th time your father brought it up? What is going on in your life right now? If you know finances are extremely tight and you are worried about making the mortgage payment, just know you will have the tendency to overreact to any slight aggravation. Knowing where you are, taking into account the environment of the conflict, will help in not only more clearly understanding our role in the conflict, but also allow a greater healing to take place.

- **Where the level stays is based upon our (and the other person's) current walk with God:**

The information given regarding the levels at which we typically respond to hurt and frustration in our lives is important to consider and realize. Also valuable to note is how our responses are triggered by our past and by others. But these deal only with the physical realm. We must address how the spiritual realm affects us and how quickly we forgive and process through the hurt done to us. The levels at which we react to our wounds and how long we remain in our anger is directly related to both our and our offender's current walk with God. As you read through the following scriptures, consider the following example and the various possible responses within this scenario. Consider a couple who has been married for 10 years, has done well financially, has three children, and are active churchgoers. Five years ago, the husband decided to purchase a condo in the city for his parents so that they would have a nice home. The parents had initially agreed to pay the monthly mortgage amount, and at the time purchased, the down payment on the condo was not a strain on the couple's finances. While there was not initial unity and complete discussion of the purchase, the real estate transaction had

LESSON 1:
WHAT IS UN-FORGIVENESS? WHAT CONTRIBUTES TO IT?

not been a source of major conflict for the couple. However, the parents got into a financial bind and stopped paying the monthly mortgage. It then became the responsibility of this couple. For a while, everything continued easily, but then the couple experienced a significant reduction in income due to a fluctuation in the economy. All of a sudden, this added monthly expense became a major strain on their budget and relationship. Because of the obligation felt by the husband to his parents, he refused to discuss any attempt to make budget changes, regardless of its necessity. This resulted in a partial level of un-forgiveness and further straining of the relationship with his wife. Using this example, let's see how different scenarios play out.

Walking in the Spirit: a righteous anger at injustice and being wronged: (Romans 12:9-21)—we return to minimal. Why?

> **Read Romans 12:9-21.**
> **Note here the marks of the true Christian.**
>
> [9] Let love be genuine. Abhor what is evil; hold fast to what is good. [10] Love one another with brotherly affection. Outdo one another in showing honor. [11] Do not be slothful in zeal, be fervent in spirit,[a] serve the Lord. [12] Rejoice in hope, be patient in tribulation, be constant in prayer. [13] Contribute to the needs of the saints and seek to show hospitality.
>
> [14] Bless those who persecute you; bless and do not curse them. [15] Rejoice with those who rejoice, weep with those who weep. [16] Live in harmony with one another. Do not be haughty, but associate with the lowly.[b] Never be wise in your own sight. [17] Repay no one evil for evil, but give thought to do what is honorable in the sight of all. [18] If possible, so far as it depends on you, live peaceably with all. [19] Beloved, never avenge yourselves, but leave it[c] to the wrath of God, for it is written, "Vengeance is mine, I will repay, says the Lord." [20] To the contrary, "if your enemy is hungry, feed him; if he is thirsty, give him something to drink; for by so doing you will heap burning coals on his head." [21] Do not be overcome by evil, but overcome evil with good.

LESSON 1:
WHAT IS UN-FORGIVENESS? WHAT CONTRIBUTES TO IT?

_____
_____
_____
_____
_____

Just because we are walking in the Spirit does not mean we will avoid being angry. Remember when we spoke about God being angry and how anger was a natural emotion given to us? Remember the Scripture telling us to be angry but not to sin in our anger? When we walk in the Spirit there will be times when righteous anger presents itself because of some injustice done or wrongdoing. However, here the wound is acknowledged, and the responding level returns to the minimal stage.

Those who choose to follow Christ are called to walk as Christ did: to love God and love one another. You know when you truly love someone else when you are at peace with them and fully allow God to hit His "mark," enacting His justice, in His own time and way. Yet, we who are Christians are told to go farther. We are even told to care for the needs of our enemies, to feed them, and give them something to drink. We are commanded to repay evil with good, which is much easier said than done. However, if both parties involved in a conflict are actively walking in the Spirit, then they will both seek peace and reconciliation. They will each realize that justice is indeed served by God and that there is no need to maintain un-forgiveness, repaying evil with evil. Rather, both parties will see the good in the situation and the good in each other. There will be a desire and willingness to work through any hurt and disagreement as well as having the goal of obtaining and seeing God's solution, God's will for this difficult situation. Therefore, the level of un-forgiveness will remain at a minimal level. Their relationship will eventually return to full release and reconciliation because they have fully recognized and embraced the heart of God wanting to bring healing and freedom to their conflict; continuing to respect and honor each other until a resolution is achieved. This results in restoration of peace and joy in the relationship, as well as complete freedom and intimacy.

In our case study, if the husband were walking in the Spirit, he would not shut down the concerns of his wife. Rather, he would openly accept and begin communications to understand the current facts of the situation and then discuss how God can provide a solution to the dilemma. Harsh words and tribulation would play no part in this, just a willingness to continue to talk and pray until God presented a solution. Neither the husband nor the wife would hold on to any anger or roots of bitterness and would never allow the situation to be "off limits."

LESSON 1:
WHAT IS UN-FORGIVENESS? WHAT CONTRIBUTES TO IT?

If we are walking in selfishness, it stays at partial or complete. Why?

_____
_____
_____
_____
_____

Because of:
- Self-will
- Self-centered
- Self-agenda

When one or both parties of a conflict are not walking in the Spirit, they are walking in selfishness, otherwise known as the flesh. When that happens, the response to a wound will be on an either partial or complete level and, unfortunately, it will become very normal for that level of un-forgiveness to remain. But what exactly is selfishness, and how can we identify it? Selfishness is defined as exercising your self-will (doing what you want to do), being self-centered (always having only your best interest at heart), and exercising your self-agenda (what is going to bring you the most happiness and prosperity). When either or both parties involved in a conflict desire their own will, focus on their own personal desires, and have only their own agenda at heart, the goal will never be to release un-forgiveness. Rather, the goal is always to maintain withholding forgiveness in order to manipulate the other person, the situation as a whole, and to ultimately achieve their desired outcome. This, of course, is not always the case. Sometimes, as you may have noticed in your own experience, the resistance to forgiveness may only be one-sided. You may be doing everything right (walking in the Spirit), but even though you may be, the other party may be walking in selfishness. If so, be forewarned. Just know their desire to live peaceably and release their self-centeredness is low, and they will continue to maintain the hurt, opposition, and frustration that serve their purposes. An integral part of gaining the freedom associated through receiving and extending forgiveness is to be honest with ourselves and God. How often are we truly walking in the Spirit? Think of all the times you experienced hurt and conflict arose. How many of those times were you walking in the Spirit? Are you walking in the Spirit now? How do you know if you are walking in the Spirit versus walking and operating in the flesh? This is a good question to which God has given us answers.

LESSON 1:
WHAT IS UN-FORGIVENESS? WHAT CONTRIBUTES TO IT?

As we stated before, we need to be able to recognize where we are coming from—spiritually speaking, that is. However, we also need to assess from where our offenders come so we can proceed with wisdom. So, what do people walking in selfishness look like?

How will an unbeliever operating without the Spirit of God normally respond?

> **Read Romans 1:18-25.**
>
> God's Wrath on Unrighteousness
> 18 For the wrath of God is revealed from heaven against all ungodliness and unrighteousness of men, who by their unrighteousness suppress the truth. 19 For what can be known about God is plain to them, because God has shown it to them. 20 For his invisible attributes, namely, his eternal power and divine nature, have been clearly perceived, ever since the creation of the world,[a] in the things that have been made. So they are without excuse. 21 For although they knew God, they did not honor him as God or give thanks to him, but they became futile in their thinking, and their foolish hearts were darkened. 22 Claiming to be wise, they became fools, 23 and exchanged the glory of the immortal God for images resembling mortal man and birds and animals and creeping things.
>
> 24 Therefore God gave them up in the lusts of their hearts to impurity, to the dishonoring of their bodies among themselves, 25 because they exchanged the truth about God for a lie and worshiped and served the creature rather than the Creator, who is blessed forever! Amen.

_____
_____
_____
_____
_____

Sin and selfishness impact everyone. As stated in the Word, all have sinned and fallen short of God's standard of perfection. In addition, His wrath is shown to those who do not worship the one true God and who squelch the truth and participate in ungodly and unrighteous acts. Unbelievers do not have the Spirit

LESSON 1:
WHAT IS UN-FORGIVENESS? WHAT CONTRIBUTES TO IT?

of God living in them, so then, why should it surprise any of us that unbelievers operate in anything other than selfishness? Without God's Spirit they are completely self-centered, absorbed in self-will and operate only within their own self-agenda. It is impossible for them to act otherwise. Because of this, they will naturally give little thought to seeking peace with others. Instead, they will typically use emotional manipulation to obtain selfish desires, regardless of how it affects or hurts others, even loved ones.

How will a believer, operating carnally, in the flesh, respond?

> **Read Romans 8:5-8.**
>
> 5 For those who live according to the flesh set their minds on the things of the flesh, but those who live according to the Spirit set their minds on the things of the Spirit. 6 For to set the mind on the flesh is death, but to set the mind on the Spirit is life and peace. 7 For the mind that is set on the flesh is hostile to God, for it does not submit to God's law; indeed, it cannot. 8 Those who are in the flesh cannot please God.

_____
_____
_____
_____
_____

> **Read James 3:14-16.**
>
> 14 But if you have bitter jealousy and selfish ambition in your hearts, do not boast and be false to the truth. 15 This is not the wisdom that comes down from above, but is earthly, unspiritual, demonic. 16 For where jealousy and selfish ambition exist, there will be disorder and every vile practice. 17 But the wisdom from above is first pure, then peaceable, gentle, open to reason, full of mercy and good fruits, impartial and sincere. 18 And a harvest of righteousness is sown in peace by those who make peace.

LESSON 1:
WHAT IS UN-FORGIVENESS? WHAT CONTRIBUTES TO IT?

_____
_____
_____
_____
_____
_____

Believers are different than unbelievers—literally as different as night and day, dark and light, life and death. We have a choice in how to live and approach conflict. According to Romans, we can choose to either walk in the Spirit or to walk in the flesh. Those who choose to walk according to the flesh have chosen to be ruled by self (self-will, self-agenda, etc.). Those who walk accordingly are arrogant, jealous, and their lives are in general disorder and full of evil. However, Christians who choose to live by the Spirit are peaceable, gentle, and the list continues.

One vital point to internalize is that our human nature dictates we do not have a neutral choice in these matters (see Romans 7:13-24). Rather, we naturally default to walking in the flesh and the self when we fail to choose to walk according to the Spirit. When we are governed by a carnal mind and are satisfying our flesh, there are three natural consequences: death of the Spirit (where we quench the Spirit, as if it were dead, and refuse to allow it to operate within and enliven us), enmity against God (where we work directly against the purposes and will of God), and the inability to please God. Consequently, maintaining un-forgiveness becomes easy when our flesh is dominant, and these consequences are running rampant in our lives. Our flesh desires to maintain un-forgiveness so we can, in turn, manipulate others to achieve our objectives. In essence, we want what we want when we want it and will do what is needed to get it. We may also happen to maintain withholding forgiveness in order to foster a constant victim mentality, which is also a foothold of the enemy. Regardless, in any of these instances where we remain in our anger, we are continually subjecting ourselves to further hurt and oppression by others.

In our earlier example, the husband continues to keep the issue of parental housing "off limits." Whenever the wife suggests they discuss finances and budgets, the husband automatically knows where the conversation is heading and shuts her down immediately. He repeatedly says he has "everything under control," that "everything will be fine," but such is not the case. In actuality, fear and anxiety only increase because the couple is not making their ends meet. The husband only gets increasingly concerned about failure and worries further about the future, not to mention refusing to address a big portion of the problem, his parents. He has found himself in a catch-22 or what's considered a classic double-bind. He has no solution. Any resolution he thinks of is inevitably going to cause further stress and strain, so he decides that no discussion is better than confrontation any day.

LESSON 1:
WHAT IS UN-FORGIVENESS? WHAT CONTRIBUTES TO IT?

In the meantime, his wife mirrors his own fears and concerns. When needing to use her disposable income strictly for the needs of the children, she swallows her anger and emotions because she knows the subject is "off limits." She uses the credit card to make purchases for the family and just endures her husband's angry outbursts when the bills inevitably come. All too soon, the ever-deepening strain and consequent edginess characterizing their relationship becomes their new normal. In this situation, both the husband and the wife are acting selfishly. Although the husband's selfishness, avoidance, and anger are easily identified, the wife's response is just as selfish. She avoids the entire issue for the same reason: she merely wants to protect herself while avoiding the conflict entirely. If either of them were actually walking in the Spirit as opposed to the flesh, they would pray and then be willing to open up for full disclosure and discuss all the facts. If the initial attempt to resolve the conflict was not received, then a third-party to assist in overcoming their "double-bind" would be needed and suggested.

> "The Father cares for your issues, your concerns, your conflicts, and especially the hearts involved."

This case study is real. We encountered it during one of the retreats Linda and I were leading. We spent much private time with this couple, helping them open up and feel safe broaching the ever-avoided issue and aid each one in communicating their emotions, thoughts, and perspectives. Just opening up the discussion in a respectful and honorable way released much of the tension and struggle in their relationship. We didn't try to fix everything at once. Instead, we focused on what could be agreed to: Their financial condition could no longer sustain the additional monthly payment. Everyone agreed change was necessary on the part of their parents—that the parents would either need to return to paying the monthly mortgage or agree to sell the property and move to a more affordable home. This couple recognized they did not have an immediate solution but acknowledged God did. And, based upon their agreement, they were willing to communicate with their parents, expressing to them the dilemma in order to bring everyone into the process of coming to a solution. We ended our time in prayer and asked God to provide His solution.

On Monday, the day after the retreat ended, we received a phone call from the wife with an amazing story. On Sunday night, the husband's parents had called and initiated discussion on the dilemma. Not only were they aware and understood the financial strain they had put upon their son, they would not allow the situation to continue! Of their own volition, his parents were very willing to consider selling the condo to purchase their own place, thus releasing the son and his wife from the financial obligation. It was obvious God had orchestrated this solution and was just waiting for the couple to release their un-forgiveness and open up a dialogue in the Spirit to come to a resolution. Such a truly remarkable work of God!

LESSON 1:
WHAT IS UN-FORGIVENESS? WHAT CONTRIBUTES TO IT?

This was a true story with a very complicated problem and a solution only God could orchestrate. This is another example that no matter your issues or conflicts, God has the solution for each and every one! The Father cares for your issues, your concerns, your conflicts, and especially the hearts involved. Will you begin the process of allowing yourself to open up a dialogue with the Spirit and allow Him to work things out in your life as well?

In situations where two or more selfish people are involved in an occurrence of hurt or dispute, these selfish people promote un-forgiveness that deepens the level of response in both. Why?

_____
_____
_____
_____
_____
_____

It should not surprise us that un-believers are selfish by nature; and thus, act in a selfish way, one that promotes hurts and wounds. Sadly, though, we must also accept that believers, too, can be selfish. We should not be surprised or ignore the effect of selfishness, which is that selfish people, believers or not, can promote un-forgiveness.

Read James 4:1-6; 4:11-12.

Warning Against Worldliness
4 What causes quarrels and what causes fights among you? Is it not this, that your passions[a] are at war within you?[b] 2 You desire and do not have, so you murder. You covet and cannot obtain, so you fight and quarrel. You do not have, because you do not ask. 3 You ask and do not receive, because you ask wrongly, to spend it on your passions. 4 You adulterous people![c] Do you not know that friendship with the world is enmity with God? Therefore whoever wishes to be a friend of the world makes himself an enemy of God. 5 Or do you suppose it is to no purpose that the Scripture says, "He yearns jealously over the spirit that he has made to dwell in us"? 6 But he gives more grace. Therefore it says, "God opposes the proud but gives grace to the humble."

LESSON 1:
WHAT IS UN-FORGIVENESS? WHAT CONTRIBUTES TO IT?

> [11] Do not speak evil against one another, brothers.[a] The one who speaks against a brother or judges his brother, speaks evil against the law and judges the law. But if you judge the law, you are not a doer of the law but a judge. [12] There is only one lawgiver and judge, he who is able to save and to destroy. But who are you to judge your neighbor?

_____
_____
_____
_____
_____

The selfish position of each asserts:

- I want…

- I really do not care about what you want…

- I am going to do…

Thus, my expectation is not met, and the other person is now a roadblock to me getting my way or doing what I want them to do for me—I am hurt, mad, and frustrated—and the level of un-forgiveness deepens.

Have you ever been in a situation where conflict arose, and both parties involved (whether they were believers or not) acted so selfishly that they somehow ended up promoting un-forgiveness? Such actions only result in deepening the level of response of all people involved. Why is that?

We all go through quarrels and disputes. But the instances where hurt and anger are maintained and not released usually result from selfish ambitions to achieve what we want rather than being actually opposed by something or someone else. These wrong motives define so much of what causes our problems in life. Selfishness is why we fight and quarrel, why we maintain our anger, and why we will work so hard to withhold forgiveness. All of these actions serve our own selfish purposes. And since most people, including many believers, daily walk in the flesh and self-centeredness, we should not be surprised in the least to witness such strained relationships and hardness of hearts. While operating in the flesh, it is nearly impossible to put others in front of yourself or see your brother as more

LESSON 1:
WHAT IS UN-FORGIVENESS? WHAT CONTRIBUTES TO IT?

important than yourself. You will stay within partial or complete un-forgiveness, and/or maintain your anger and hostility. Within disputes, each person comes into the argument with his own selfish desires: "I want…," "I could really care less about what you want…," "and I am going to do whatever I need to…," etc. In these situations, neither party has his needs met, and both focus on how they are "hurt," "angry," or "haven't been heard," and the wound deepens even more. And, it does not stop there. Within this selfishness, there are underlying contributors to un-forgiveness that tend to deepen the level at which we operate:

Normal:

- Difference in personality.

God made us with a great variety of personalities, and we are naturally attracted to others with differing personalities that complement our own. However, as we get closer to and more intimate with these people we were initially attracted to, we find that those personality differences become irritating. For example, I am naturally aggressive and a risk taker. Linda, my spouse, is naturally verbal and risk-avoidant. We had an opportunity to invest in a new venture, which to me looked good. Because of my personality, I was willing to take the risk and wasn't worried if it did not work out. Linda, on the other hand, being risk averse, did not want to make the investment. Because of our personality differences, we found ourselves in conflict. It wasn't due to any real difference of opinion, but rather our normal differences in personality. Before we understood this natural difference, we would battle and argue just because we disagreed. These disagreements accentuated our personality differences, naturally making things more difficult. If you were to take out all other stimuli and factors, we should know that we will continually be prone to conflict simply due to the differences in our personalities! If we do not choose to walk in the Spirit, natural personality differences can deepen any level of un-forgiveness if left unchecked.

We also must consider that we have differences of opinion about ways of living life including money, marriage, children, career, friends, time, holidays, travel, relatives, sex, ministry, etc.

We all come from different backgrounds, all of which shape how we live life. We have all learned differing ways to approach everyday issues. Since we were raised with different viewpoints on how to spend money, roles within marriage, how to raise children, etc., they can become stress points of natural conflict. Just because your friend or spouse, your boss or co-worker have completely different views of career goals, how to spend the holidays, what to do with relatives,

LESSON 1:
WHAT IS UN-FORGIVENESS? WHAT CONTRIBUTES TO IT?

> "Walking in the Spirit will help to avoid deepening any level of un-forgiveness."

doesn't mean they are wrong. Their views are simply different. This particularly comes out in political discussion. Linda and I had a retreat in Europe where the discussion drifted to political parties and how could Christians be on such different sides of the political spectrum. Linda and I had already worked through our understanding that people have different views of life, and therefore it was not worth debating these different views (while it is okay to discuss what we think, we should not allow our differences to cause arguments, debates, or hard feelings). Others, having not worked through this, experienced those harsh feelings, which inevitably arose and consequently brought deeper levels of un-forgiveness. We helped them work through and release those feelings, to understand that different views of life are normal and not something that should contribute to conflict and anger. But, knowing these differences serve as a warning when having to come to an agreement on an issue. Be mindful that these are natural conflict areas—they are normal and should be expected. Walking in the Spirit will help to avoid deepening any level of un-forgiveness.

Abnormal:

- Continuing unmet expectations
- Guilt
- Purposeful hurt
- Lack of follow through
- Wounds

These are contributing factors that are not caused by normal differences we all encounter, but rather are things caused by our selfish nature. They might be considered a normal part of life (we experience them often in our world); but they are not part of God's intention of how He wants life to be lived. In these situations, we wind up in an "oppressive state," causing us to carry around continual anger. Then, when something happens to cause hurt or frustration, we over react, our anger deepens, and our oppression gets heavier. Some of these are as follows:

- **Continuing unmet expectations.** Disappointment and resignation can quickly lead to un-forgiveness when our expectations about what we thought life was going to be are not met.

- **Guilt.** When you cannot get over the things done in the past, it leads us to withhold forgiveness, especially toward ourselves.

LESSON 1:
WHAT IS UN-FORGIVENESS? WHAT CONTRIBUTES TO IT?

- **Wounds.** These are deep patterns of behavior from our past which, when the buttons are pushed by a variety of circumstances, cause our unhealthy responses.

- **Other people's interactions with us:**

  - **Purposeful hurt.** Often, people know what we want, but are striving for and purposefully opposed to us and come against it. This could be done either directly or passive-aggressively.

  - **Lack of follow through.** When someone said they would do something for us but do not keep their promise or perform the stated task on time or with excellence.

At one of our retreats, we had a couple who had experienced life with all of these abnormal stressors operating at once. They had not been able to find enjoyable career positions and were bouncing from job to job. As a result, they had gone into credit card debt and were under a heavy financial burden. Their life together had been a whirlwind of continuing unmet expectations, and they had developed a rather negative view of life, which usually reflected a low view of God and an actual deep anger and un–forgiveness of God. They did not expect good things to happen to them and could not even imagine or dream of such. Furthermore, they had stopped attending church and spending time in God's Word, so they carried a level of guilt knowing their life was not pleasing to God. The truth was: They were mad at God, they didn't want to spend any time with Him, but because they were believers, they carried guilt about not wanting to spend time with their Father. To complicate matters further, one of their bosses was particularly harsh and power mad and would continually do things to purposely hurt and oppress his employees. Even though they were rightfully frustrated and angry at the boss, it only intensified their negative view of life. Adding insult to injury, one of their projects achieved a key milestone and even though they were promised a bonus, the company did not honor its commitment. This became a further sore spot of anger toward their boss and the company. When this was paired with deep childhood wounds of parental disappointments, they were living in an atmosphere of guilt, lack of follow through, and an expectation of being inevitably let down.

When they finally understood the un-forgiveness they carried from all these things, which also reflected the oppression of everyday life, they agreed to learn to abide in the Word and experience the release of un-forgiveness and the freshness of the new life. It was not a single event or an automatic transformation, but a day-

LESSON 1:
WHAT IS UN-FORGIVENESS? WHAT CONTRIBUTES TO IT?

by-day, month-by-month process where God changed them internally and then changed circumstances externally to fulfill all that He wanted to do in their lives. This was truly another remarkable example of God's power.

Though we have covered the "normal" and "abnormal" factors which contribute to how we respond to wounds, there is yet another: spiritual attack from the enemy.

> **Read Ephesians 6:11-12.**
>
> [11] Put on the whole armor of God, that you may be able to stand against the schemes of the devil. [12] For we do not wrestle against flesh and blood, but against the rulers, against the authorities, against the cosmic powers over this present darkness, against the spiritual forces of evil in the heavenly places.

We know the enemy uses various schemes and strategies to deepen our anger, to cause us hurt, and to encourage our revengeful thinking.

Spiritual attacks stand uniquely different. They are normal because the enemy is alive, well, and wants to make us live apart from the Spirit. Spiritual attacks are abnormal because they do not operate in what we typically experience with our five senses. Spiritual attacks, being very different by nature, also require a different approach in how to withstand them. We must recall that we are fighting against powers and principalities and not flesh and blood, and then must understand many of the things that happen in life are direct spiritual attacks from the enemy— with the goal of moving us to un-forgiveness and thus, bondage and oppression.

There are schemes and strategies of the devil. The enemy is alive and very real. The enemy has strategies and schemes to directly affect you. The enemy's goal is to steal, kill, and destroy. This includes your heart. He will do anything he can in order to deepen your anger, hurt others, and get you to exact your own revenge by doing any or all of the following:

- Pushing your buttons that intensify wounds of past

- Escalating raw feelings

- Causing miscommunications

- Ensuring misinterpretations

LESSON 1:
WHAT IS UN-FORGIVENESS? WHAT CONTRIBUTES TO IT?

- Piling on stress and negative circumstances

- Creating distractions so that we never get to talk or resolve the negativity, which causes it to go deeper by default.

Because we're such poor communicators (usually because we don't have or take the time), the enemy's schemes are rather easy to carry out. At one of our retreats, a wife commented that she was tired. The husband heard that she was "sick and tired," and interpreted that to mean she was angry at him for not taking care of their finances. He then became defensive and attempted to rationalize what he was doing financially for the family. She became angry because he disregarded her weariness and physical exhaustion. Their issue escalated into deeper arguing and debating—all because they didn't "hear" the same words spoken (i.e., miscommunication). As we helped this couple unpack their miscommunication, many factors came to light. We all discovered that the husband lived in fear when it came to his finances and projected this fear and anxiety onto his wife. His wife? Well, she was just weary from taking care of two small children without respite and missed the ability to spend time alone as a couple. Through careful communication we were able to counteract the work of the enemy who would have taken the simple miscommunication even further into deeper levels of un-forgiveness in anger. We all realized then, and now, how clever the enemy is and how important it is to continually process what we hear from each other so we do not give any ground to the enemy.

Take an honest assessment of your wounds, your scars, all of your unchecked anger. Were there examples in your past, or even right now, where personality differences contributed to an otherwise simple difference of opinion? Was guilt a player in how you snapped at your spouse last week? Are your expectations on your child's education unhealthy because of your wounded past? Did the enemy twist a rather basic miscommunication into something worse, turning it into an attack? Try to assess the environment of the wounds that are the most pressing on your heart right now and sincerely ask the Father to reveal to you what else contributed to the conflict other than the words said. Then, be willing to receive the truth He will reveal to you as you continue in your journey toward the freedom granted in forgiveness.

LESSON 1:
WHAT IS UN-FORGIVENESS? WHAT CONTRIBUTES TO IT?

With the person and/or persons that I am having some un-forgiveness toward, what are some of the normal and abnormal reasons that are operating in me and in these situations?

_____
_____
_____
_____
_____
_____
_____

Where is the enemy working with his schemes and strategies to intensify the anger and the conflict of these situations?

_____
_____
_____
_____
_____
_____
_____

What insight have these verses given me regarding where my responses are and the explanation for my responses?

_____
_____
_____
_____
_____
_____
_____
_____

LESSON 1:
WHAT IS UN-FORGIVENESS? WHAT CONTRIBUTES TO IT?

LESSON 2:
WHY WE WITHHOLD FORGIVENESS

When you take into account everything we've discussed so far and reflect upon the words and meaning, why do we continue to hold on to un-forgiveness? Why is it so difficult to move beyond the hurt and merely forgive? Why do we choose to punish ourselves in retaining our anger and animosity and keep our hearts imprisoned when Christ came to set us free?

> **Read Romans 1:26-32.**
>
> 26 For this reason God gave them up to dishonorable passions. For their women exchanged natural relations for those that are contrary to nature; 27 and the men likewise gave up natural relations with women and were consumed with passion for one another, men committing shameless acts with men and receiving in themselves the due penalty for their error.
>
> 28 And since they did not see fit to acknowledge God, God gave them up to a debased mind to do what ought not to be done. 29 They were filled with all manner of unrighteousness, evil, covetousness, malice. They are full of envy, murder, strife, deceit, maliciousness. They are gossips, 30 slanderers, haters of God, insolent, haughty, boastful, inventors of evil, disobedient to parents, 31 foolish, faithless, heartless, ruthless. 32 Though they know God's righteous decree that those who practice such things deserve to die, they not only do them but give approval to those who practice them.

> "We are so wounded and have been for so long that we have retrained our minds to shy away from any type of constructive criticism."

_____
_____
_____
_____
_____
_____

LESSON 2:
WHY WE WITHHOLD FORGIVENESS

When our anger deepens, it turns into bitterness and strife. We are found without understanding and thus become creatures that do not love, do not show mercy, and do not forgive. Our emotions are completely unstable and are anything but neutral. Unless we are walking according to the Spirit, such fleshly actions and selfishness will only become worse, indeed more acute, and our un-forgiveness will follow suit. This is why our society is the way it is. Un-forgiveness is running rampant in our world and has resulted in a pandemic of wounded, broken, and bleeding individuals who show no mercy or hope. We show no hope because, when we choose to hold on to our own ways and refuse to forgive, we have failed to receive hope from the Giver of Life. Even believers, who have been so beautifully forgiven, refuse to forgive others because they do not walk in God's Spirit and in His love.

Review some of the reasons we tend to hold on to un-forgiveness:

- Hurts and pain are so deep that they never get to healing.

People are in pain, real pain, and many times such pain and deep wounds are too deep to reach without forgiveness. You see, with forgiveness, true healing can be experienced and without it, our wounds continue to rot, and the disease of self clutches all the more firmly.

- I am so poor at handling conflict (rarely get anywhere and tend to be out maneuvered) and find that it is much easier to avoid conflict than deal with it. Over time, this pattern of avoiding conflict becomes my normal way of handling things. I just live with it.

We are so wounded and have been for so long that we have retrained our minds to shy away from any type of constructive criticism. The lessons we have learned along the way have taught us that quite clearly. "It is much easier to avoid conflict altogether and sweep it under the rug than to fully resolve the issues," we chant over and over in our minds, eventually believing the lie. We tell ourselves that even if we did try to resolve any conflict, we would be out-maneuvered, or it would just turn into another fight, so why even try? The danger of this thinking is that these patterns eventually cement themselves into your brain and become your new norm, the normal way you live your life and handle any and all current and future conflict. You resign yourself to the fact that you must simply "live with it." It is here that the hope of believing there is anything better slowly dies.

LESSON 2:
WHY WE WITHHOLD FORGIVENESS

HOW WE CONFUSE FORGIVENESS WITH RECONCILATION:

The most prevalent reason we withhold forgiveness is: WE CONFUSE FORGIVENESS WITH RECONCILIATION. We think that forgiveness means that I am "reconciling to" or "accepting" fully regarding all that a person has done to hurt or offend me. Unless that person has admitted to what they have done and then apologized, this reconciliation means that I am now accepting what they have done as okay without them having to deal with the injustice of what they have done. So, unless the other party is willing to process through to "real" reconciliation, I can't get to "real" forgiveness. This is a difficult concept, one that we will help clear up in the next few chapters.

Because of this confusion, my thinking is that: If I forgive, I incorrectly believe that:

I will never be able to share my real feelings, hurts, pain, and anger.

I may stimulate further conflict with the other person who may be stronger than me (in personality, in emotion, in hostility, in authority, and power over me—either formally or historically, i.e., with a mother or father, even though I am an adult), and I will just make things worse. It is simply too much trouble.

I will reinforce that what the other person did is okay, and they never have to deal with or have any consequences to what they did. They will only get stronger in their selfishness.

I end up sanctioning and promoting the other person doing this again to me—in fact, over and over again to me.

By holding on to my un-forgiveness, I control the dynamics. I make sure these things that I believe do not happen. Actually, by maintaining my coldness and distance in un-forgiveness, I believe that I am:

- Protecting my heart from further hurts and pains.

- Making a statement that what the other person did was wrong, and the other person should feel:

LESSON 2:
WHY WE WITHHOLD FORGIVENESS

- Guilt

- My disapproval

- Sad at our changed relationship

- That I no longer will not allow the other person to do this again easily and keep hurting me. This deadens my pain and allows me to scab over my wounds.

- The consequences of not having me serve you and miss out on the benefits of our past relationship.

- My need to function by avoiding conflict and by setting up walls around me to protect me.

Actually, what is happening to my heart is quite the opposite (write out the truth of these verses):

> **Read Proverbs 14:10.**
>
> [10] The heart knows its own bitterness, and no stranger shares its joy.

_____
_____
_____
_____
_____

> **Read Ephesians 4:30-31.**
>
> [30] And do not grieve the Holy Spirit of God, by whom you were sealed for the day of redemption. [31] Let all bitterness and wrath and anger and clamor and slander be put away from you, along with all malice.

LESSON 2:
WHY WE WITHHOLD FORGIVENESS

_____
_____
_____
_____
_____
_____

> **Read Hebrews 12:15.**
>
> [15] See to it that no one fails to obtain the grace of God; that no "root of bitterness" springs up and causes trouble, and by it many become defiled.

_____
_____
_____
_____
_____
_____

> **Read Jeremiah 17:5-6; 17:9.**
>
> [5] Thus says the Lord:
> "Cursed is the man who trusts in man
>   and makes flesh his strength,[a]
>   whose heart turns away from the Lord.
> [6] He is like a shrub in the desert,
>   and shall not see any good come.
> He shall dwell in the parched places of the wilderness,
>   in an uninhabited salt land.
>
> [9] The heart is deceitful above all things,
>   and desperately sick;
>   who can understand it?

LESSON 2:
WHY WE WITHHOLD FORGIVENESS

_____
_____
_____
_____
_____

There are other wounds and issues in my life that contribute to my inability to go to forgiveness: (Write descriptions of what they are and how they are impacting your life at the moment.)

_____
_____
_____
_____

Up to this point, we may have tried to convince ourselves that withholding forgiveness to those who have wounded us actually protects us, but that is a lie. God's Word says that as we continually walk in the flesh and operate in the carnal self, we experience the three consequences listed in Romans 8:5-8: death of the Spirit, enmity against God, and the inability to please God. It's as if we operate as there were no God, and believers operate as practical atheists. Our hearts subsequently move deeper into un-forgiveness, and the emotions we experience or think we control actually cause:

- Deepening of Wounds
- Roots of Bitterness
- Edginess
- Frustration
- Low-grade Anger
- Short Fuses, Triggers, and Hot-buttons
- A feeling of being locked up, in bondage
- Negativity in our energy or outlook; critical feelings

LESSON 2:
WHY WE WITHHOLD FORGIVENESS

> "Un-forgiveness is literally the root of Christians living in bondage, oppression, and unhappiness instead of the fullness of all Christ promised."

Un-forgiveness is literally the root of Christians living in bondage, oppression, and unhappiness instead of the fullness of all Christ promised. Our world is becoming more and more stressful, as we are bombarded by selfishness and messages that we are to live in such a way to get what you deserve (and if we don't go after what is rightfully ours, we will be doormats and open for continual abuse). We have accepted that living in un-forgiveness is normal. Because of the dysfunctions of our families, our work, our friendships—even our church communities, we are continually wounded and hurt; and angry with roots of bitterness. While it seems difficult to even think that we can reach a modest level of forgiveness toward those who have hurt us, we mostly hold on to un-forgiveness because of the misunderstanding that if I forgive, I am accepting the continual hurt, and the only way to get to forgiveness is to have those who hurt us get to a place of acceptable reconciliation—admitting what they have done and agreeing to discontinue these harmful acts toward me. We actually use it as a tool to establish a wall that we think is protecting our hearts and souls, and the circumstances of our life. What we don't understand is that it is causing us great pain, even physical problems, certainly mental and spiritual difficulties, and we are not enjoying the abundant life promised to us by our Lord Jesus. As we do gain this understanding, let us pursue God's truth that can free us from this awful situation.

Look at your life and your attitude toward life as a whole. How would you define it? Do you experience joy, peace, and general order? Do you generally live in fear and are critical of others? Does your life reflect the promises of Scripture for those who walk in the Spirit, or does it look quite the opposite? Be honest with yourself, because the fruit of living in the Spirit cannot be falsely generated. If you are not enjoying the abundant life Christ promised to His children, then begin to look at un-forgiveness in your life. Against whom do you hold grudges or hostility? Who are you icy toward or roll your eyes at when they walk into the room? Start with the obvious ones and then allow the Spirit to guide you into further truth as you begin to look at forgiving that high school teacher, the college roommate, your uncle, your boss.

Write what you have learned about why you tend to hold on to "un-forgiveness" and where the Lord wants to bring healing and restoration. Journal your thoughts and feelings about these issues and what the Lord is speaking to you about these.

_____
_____
_____
_____

LESSON 2:
WHY WE WITHHOLD FORGIVENESS

LESSON 3:
WHAT IS FORGIVENESS? (PART 1)

> "When you forgive, you are releasing your anger against your offender and have decided to terminate all resentment toward them."

Dictionary definition: Compassionate feelings that allow a person to pardon another: release and conclude resentment, indignation, or anger as a result of a perceived offense, difference, or mistake.

These feelings and ability to pardon another come from God. In fact, it is GOD HIMSELF—His nature! His nature is grace and compassion that releases the wrath and anger that we all deserve because of what we have done, this, as we know, is SIN.

Before we jump right into defining what forgiveness is, I want to give a very practical example from my own life. Do you remember when I was discussing my relationship with my mother? Through that strained relationship God revealed to me what bondage and oppression look like when dealing with unforgiveness. He also reminded me that I had an example from my past of what true forgiveness looks like.

In college, I worked for an advertising company and was responsible for compiling all materials needed for use in client presentations, (remember, these were the days before computers, so all the materials were hard copy). Because I continually demonstrated competence in completing projects, the partners began trusting my ability to correctly execute given assignments. One project, where we all were working toward securing a big client, I received an assignment requiring a very lengthy and complex list of materials to be complied for an important meeting. The presentation package was put together, and I treated it like the rest of my projects at the time and believed it to be correct. The day before the presentation, one of the partners asked me to verify that all of the information was correct. He asked me to get back to him once I had finished checking. I said I would call him back. However, the next day I had a term paper due and needed to stay up late to complete it. Since I assumed the packet was correct, I did not take the extra time to physically doublecheck my work. Yet, I called the partner anyway and told him everything was in order. The next day during the presentation, the final three slides, the "punchline" of the entire meeting, were missing. Not only were the partners not able to illustrate their creative approach to their client, they also presented themselves as an agency that could not pay attention to details. Needless to say, my company lost

LESSON 3:
WHAT IS FORGIVENESS? (PART 1)

that account, and the fault rested squarely upon my shoulders. I failed to fulfill my assignment on top of lying about verifying my work. I had every right to be fired. Yet, I was shown forgiveness and grace. When one of the partners called me into his office, he discussed how my lack of integrity affected him, his business integrity, as well as the integrity of the agency. Then he said he was giving me a gift in keeping my job, that he believed I would learn a valuable life lesson as a result of this mistake. He encouraged me to leave my mistake behind me and only look forward to becoming the best I could be. Instead of firing me, he gave me even more responsibility! What an amazing example of forgiveness, a wonderful demonstration of what forgiveness really looks like.

In light of this story from my past, I ask you: What exactly is forgiveness? What are the true dimensions of forgiveness? What does it feel like? We can start to explain forgiveness by saying it includes having compassionate feelings toward a person who wronged you, and these feelings allow you to pardon them. But forgiveness is more than mere feelings. When you forgive, you are releasing your anger against your offender and have decided to terminate all resentment toward them. So, all of that indignation and anger that bubbled up as the result of difference of opinions or a simple mistake or offense no longer are held against your wrongdoer. You decide to let it go; you choose not to hold on to the offense any longer. Remember the agency partner? He addressed my mistakes, reminded me that those mistakes were worthy of causing termination, and told me to learn from them. Not only that, but he chose not to hold those against me and encouraged me to not hold them against myself, to move on, and simply use my mistakes as a springboard for becoming even better. Those feelings of compassion that allowed him to forgive me and that allow you to likewise forgive others, come from God Himself. In fact, God's very nature is the compassion and grace He freely bestows upon us. We are the ones who deserve the wrath and anger of God because of the sin we have committed, but God releases that wrath and no longer holds it against us. God forgives us and, simply, lets our sin go.

What are the elements of forgiveness as defined by these verses?

> **Read Psalm 130:3-4; 130:7.**
>
> [3] If you, O Lord, should mark iniquities,
>   O Lord, who could stand?
> [4] But with you there is forgiveness,
>   that you may be feared.

LESSON 3:
WHAT IS FORGIVENESS? (PART 1)

> ⁷ O Israel, hope in the Lord!
> For with the Lord there is steadfast love,
> and with him is plentiful redemption.

Read Psalm 103:8-12.

> ⁸ The Lord is merciful and gracious,
> slow to anger and abounding in steadfast love.
> ⁹ He will not always chide,
> nor will he keep his anger forever.
> ¹⁰ He does not deal with us according to our sins,
> nor repay us according to our iniquities.
> ¹¹ For as high as the heavens are above the earth,
> so great is his steadfast love toward those who fear him;
> ¹² as far as the east is from the west,
> so far does he remove our transgressions from us.

LESSON 3:
WHAT IS FORGIVENESS? (PART 1)

> **God is eternally holy—perfectly righteous. Read Isaiah 6:3.**
>
> ³ And one called to another and said:
> "Holy, holy, holy is the Lord of hosts;
> the whole earth is full of his glory!"[a]

> **Read Revelation 4:8-11.**
>
> ⁸ And the four living creatures, each of them with six wings, are full of eyes all around and within, and day and night they never cease to say,
> "Holy, holy, holy, is the Lord God Almighty,
>   who was and is and is to come!"
> ⁹ And whenever the living creatures give glory and honor and thanks to him who is seated on the throne, who lives forever and ever, ¹⁰ the twenty-four elders fall down before him who is seated on the throne and worship him who lives forever and ever. They cast their crowns before the throne, saying,
> ¹¹ "Worthy are you, our Lord and God,
> to receive glory and honor and power,
> for you created all things,
> and by your will they existed and were created."

LESSON 3:
WHAT IS FORGIVENESS? (PART 1)

When Scripture speaks of holiness, it means something or someone is wholly distinct, separate, in a class all by themselves. R. C. Sproul explains it this way in his book, *The Holiness of God*:

> The primary meaning of holy is "separate." It comes from an ancient word that meant, "to cut," or "to separate." Perhaps even more accurate would be the phrase "a cut above something." When we find a garment or another piece of merchandise that is outstanding, that has a superior excellence, we use the expression that it is "a cut above the rest."

So, God is unique and has no rivals or competition. He is completely other than anyone or anything else in all creation. But God's holiness encompasses so much more. God's holiness also means He is worthy of all honor and power and glory (praise, fame, and/or adoration). If God is worth such accolades, which we call worship, He must also be pure, having no wrong or evil in Him—which is true! God is good, He is morally pure, He loves perfectly and is perfect love, and every action He does is the same. God is the only perfect being, and since He is perfectly righteous (morally upright and above reproach) to forgive others as He has forgiven us certainly is divine.

Take a minute to let all these wonderful truths sink into your head and heart. The last thing you need to do is to rush past the truths contained within these Scriptures. Ask yourself, what does it mean to me that God's very nature is to forgive? How does this one statement change your perception of God and your relationship with Him? When you begin to grasp this reality, it makes more sense to also embrace how God is truly other, wholly different than the humanity He created. Only the One who is wholly different, who is holy, can have a nature defined by forgiveness. This forgiveness, spurred on by His never ending love toward His children, is waiting for you to receive it. Spend ample time letting these statements become truth to you, become life for you, and thank the Father for His nature.

God's Original Plan

This holy and wholly other and different God delighted in creating, and still does! So, when God created Adam and Eve in the garden, He created them perfectly. They were holy as He is holy, perfect, and righteous. He created them to have an exceptional life and constant communion with Himself. God created man to have a full and enjoyable relationship with their Creator.

LESSON 3:
WHAT IS FORGIVENESS? (PART 1)

Read Genesis 1:26-2:25.

26 Then God said, "Let us make man[a] in our image, after our likeness. And let them have dominion over the fish of the sea and over the birds of the heavens and over the livestock and over all the earth and over every creeping thing that creeps on the earth."

27 So God created man in his own image,
 in the image of God he created him;
 male and female he created them.

28 And God blessed them. And God said to them, "Be fruitful and multiply and fill the earth and subdue it, and have dominion over the fish of the sea and over the birds of the heavens and over every living thing that moves on the earth." 29 And God said, "Behold, I have given you every plant yielding seed that is on the face of all the earth, and every tree with seed in its fruit. You shall have them for food. 30 And to every beast of the earth and to every bird of the heavens and to everything that creeps on the earth, everything that has the breath of life, I have given every green plant for food." And it was so. 31 And God saw everything that he had made, and behold, it was very good. And there was evening and there was morning, the sixth day.

The Seventh Day, God Rests
2 Thus the heavens and the earth were finished, and all the host of them. 2 And on the seventh day God finished his work that he had done, and he rested on the seventh day from all his work that he had done. 3 So God blessed the seventh day and made it holy, because on it God rested from all his work that he had done in creation.

The Creation of Man and Woman
4 These are the generations
of the heavens and the earth when they were created,
in the day that the Lord God made the earth and the heavens.

5 When no bush of the field[b] was yet in the land[c] and no small plant of the field had yet sprung up—for the Lord God had not caused it to rain on the land, and there was no man to work the ground, 6 and a mist[d] was going up from

LESSON 3:
WHAT IS FORGIVENESS? (PART 1)

the land and was watering the whole face of the ground— [7] then the Lord God formed the man of dust from the ground and breathed into his nostrils the breath of life, and the man became a living creature. [8] And the Lord God planted a garden in Eden, in the east, and there he put the man whom he had formed. [9] And out of the ground the Lord God made to spring up every tree that is pleasant to the sight and good for food. The tree of life was in the midst of the garden, and the tree of the knowledge of good and evil.

[10] A river flowed out of Eden to water the garden, and there it divided and became four rivers. [11] The name of the first is the Pishon. It is the one that flowed around the whole land of Havilah, where there is gold. [12] And the gold of that land is good; bdellium and onyx stone are there. [13] The name of the second river is the Gihon. It is the one that flowed around the whole land of Cush. [14] And the name of the third river is the Tigris, which flows east of Assyria. And the fourth river is the Euphrates.

[15] The Lord God took the man and put him in the garden of Eden to work it and keep it. [16] And the Lord God commanded the man, saying, "You may surely eat of every tree of the garden, [17] but of the tree of the knowledge of good and evil you shall not eat, for in the day that you eat[e] of it you shall surely die."
[18] Then the Lord God said, "It is not good that the man should be alone; I will make him a helper fit for[f] him." [19] Now out of the ground the Lord God had formed[g] every beast of the field and every bird of the heavens and brought them to the man to see what he would call them. And whatever the man called every living creature, that was its name. [20] The man gave names to all livestock and to the birds of the heavens and to every beast of the field. But for Adam[h] there was not found a helper fit for him. [21] So the Lord God caused a deep sleep to fall upon the man, and while he slept took one of his ribs and closed up its place with flesh. [22] And the rib that the Lord God had taken from the man he made[i] into a woman and brought her to the man. [23] Then the man said,

"This at last is bone of my bones
  and flesh of my flesh;
she shall be called Woman,
  because she was taken out of Man."[j]
[24] Therefore a man shall leave his father and his mother and hold fast to his wife, and they shall become one flesh. [25] And the man and his wife were both naked and were not ashamed.

LESSON 3:
WHAT IS FORGIVENESS? (PART 1)

God's original plan and intention for His most beloved creations, man and woman, were for them to live in perpetual beauty on the Earth. Upon this Earth was everything needed for them not only to merely exist, but to flourish amidst everything pleasing to the eye. When God creates something, He indeed shows off His power and creativity. God wanted mankind to have exceptional life. This exceptional life included extraordinary authority. Adam and Eve were charged by God to control the Earth and to rule over all the animals. They were to do so in a caring manner that would lead to greater flocks and herds, as well as cultivating more abundant and fruitful trees and other growing plants. This was also remarkable work to do. God was entrusting Adam and Eve with the rest of His creation! That is quite a charge upon them.

They were to experience exceptional work—not tedious or laborious. In the beginning, work was good and profitable and even enjoyable. Not only were they created to have amazing authority and work, but within that authority and work was exceptional provision. Everything they could possibly want or need was laid before them in Eden. There was an abundance of ripe and juicy fruit, vegetables, nuts, and roots for them to feast upon each and every day. God not only gave them enough to survive upon, He provided Adam and Eve more than they would ever need. And God gave Adam and Eve the charge together to enjoy an exceptional marriage. They were married to one another and so had the shared responsibility of tending God's entire creation. Not only did God present a helpmate suitable to Adam at the appropriate time, He did so from a bone intended to guard Adam's heart. This is quite a picture. Woman's original purpose was to become such a helper to her husband that she not only helped guard his heart, but she would be indispensable in his life, to always be at his side, wherever he went. Two people operating as one flesh: in agreement on purpose, direction, intention, and heart-in-hand. This was an exceptional marriage. There was no shame, no guilt, no past to worry about on either side. They were free to find pleasure in each other and in each other's company with no jealousy or divided attentions. They were free to enjoy their relationship with all of creation and relish their exceptional identity they had been given. What was this unique and remarkable identity? They were God's pet project: the only creation made by God's hands, given the breath of God, the only one made in His image. They were image bearers of the Creator and walked among the rest of creation as the representation of God. Everything Adam did reflected the will and desire of his Creator, but it was always under the authority of God Almighty. Adam and Eve each had the unique ability and identity to represent God in both His nature and His desired task upon the Earth.

And how did they know so clearly God's design for them within all of creation? That has everything to do with their extraordinary relationship with the Creator

LESSON 3:
WHAT IS FORGIVENESS? (PART 1)

of the heavens and Earth. There was absolutely nothing in the beginning that would hinder the exceptional communion experienced between Creator and creation. Later in Genesis, Scripture states how God walked in the cool of the day with Adam. God walked with them! When you or I walk with someone on a consistent basis, we rarely do so in silence. Some of the best conversations can be experienced while walking with another because in those moments you are sharing life along with sharing strides. Laughing becomes commonplace as you may reminisce of past memories or jokes and dreaming the big dreams seems nearly attainable when you have a friend by your side, encouraging you along the path. God had an intimate relationship with His beloved man and woman, fully intending that such a relationship would be available and desired by all forthcoming generations. It was in these early days that Adam and Eve naturally walked each day guided by the Spirit, because the very Spirit of God was resident with them. All three parts of their humanity—the flesh (material), the soul (the seat of the personality, will, intellect, and emotions), and the Spirit—were all of one accord. Unfortunately, things did not stay in such beautiful harmony for long.

Such beauty and such harmony can make one's soul ache for that which has been lost. Our spirits know that we have lost what was originally intended for us by our Heavenly Father, but this is not the time to dwell on past failures. It is the time to be thankful for God's original intention for us! His intentions for us remain the same, even though we are not created as Adam and Eve. Dream for a bit: What would your life look like if this very same authority, provision, enjoyable work, marriage, and identity were offered to you right now? What if you had them right now? Let your soul dare to dream this God-sized dream and become like a child once again. Daydream about riding on elephants, about grapes the size of a fist, swimming with sharks without fear. Whatever it is, fantasize about God's original intentions and start hoping for the future!

Our Failing and Falling

When God created the garden and the first humans in perfection, He told Adam and Eve they could eat of any tree except for the tree of the knowledge of good and evil. Remember, Eden is said to have had four rivers coming together in it. Although the exact size of Eden is unsure, we can assume it was quite expansive. This being said, there was a plethora of fruit-bearing trees for man and woman to eat from, and only one tree to avoid. Even with myriads of choices for food, Adam and Even chose to eat of that tree, against the will of God, and because of their willful act of the flesh, they sinned. This changed everything.

Adam and Eve exercised self-will and disobeyed God—choosing to eat of the tree of the knowledge of good and evil. This was mankind's first SIN (the exercise of self-will against the will of God).

LESSON 3:
WHAT IS FORGIVENESS? (PART 1)

> **Read Genesis 3:1-7.**
>
> The Fall
> **3** Now the serpent was more crafty than any other beast of the field that the Lord God had made.
>
> He said to the woman, "Did God actually say, 'You[a] shall not eat of any tree in the garden'?" **2** And the woman said to the serpent, "We may eat of the fruit of the trees in the garden, **3** but God said, 'You shall not eat of the fruit of the tree that is in the midst of the garden, neither shall you touch it, lest you die.'" **4** But the serpent said to the woman, "You will not surely die. **5** For God knows that when you eat of it your eyes will be opened, and you will be like God, knowing good and evil." **6** So when the woman saw that the tree was good for food, and that it was a delight to the eyes, and that the tree was to be desired to make one wise,[b] she took of its fruit and ate, and she also gave some to her husband who was with her, and he ate. **7** Then the eyes of both were opened, and they knew that they were naked. And they sewed fig leaves together and made themselves loincloths.

Yes, Adam and Eve were deceived and tempted by the serpent, and no, they could not have prevented the temptation from happening. However, they still chose to go against God's command regarding the fruit. This decision, this disobedience, caused them to perish. This act caused their spirit to literally die. That wonderful Spirit-given holiness and perfect righteousness originally imparted by God was now gone forever. The sweet communion they had previously shared with God was also severed, and they found themselves forever separated from a Holy God. Sin had killed their spirit and allowed physical death to creep in as well. Because of their sin, their exercise of self-will, they fully deserved God's eternal wrath and anger because the creation had deeply wronged the Holy Creator. But we know the story does not end there. Hope still exists.

Since God's very nature is forgiveness, He did not eternally separate *Himself* from *His* creation by demanding us to achieve perfection and holiness on our own. God knew we could not achieve such a demand. He knew this inability on our part would result in eternal separation. So, He gave Moses the law. In the law, the sin issue was addressed through sacrificing a perfect lamb by the High Priest. This was done every year on the Day of Atonement. Through the shedding of innocent blood, through the killing of an innocent lamb, the sin of Israel was atoned for, or satisfied, repaired, and reconciled (Leviticus 16-17). But, the essence of the law was

LESSON 3:
WHAT IS FORGIVENESS? (PART 1)

ultimately to remind mankind they cannot remedy their sin by themselves, and the lamb's sacrifice was a foreshadowing of the last Lamb to be killed for humanity.

Many of us are overly familiar with the story of the Garden of Eden, the snake, the fruit, etc. In our over-familiarity of this story, we can sometimes become immune to the gravity of sin in history and sin in our own lives. Make no mistake, sin and eternal separation from God are both real and painful to the heart of our Father. His nature is to forgive, but because He is holy, He cannot allow imperfection into His presence. This proves a problem. How can a Holy God reconcile Himself to imperfect humanity? The answer is through forgiveness. But this goes way beyond following a set of laws, way beyond doing our "best," and it has everything to do with a Lamb. If you have never acknowledged your sinfulness to God, do it now. Accept the fact that you aren't perfect and are in good company for not being perfect! Remember, none of us is. However, there is hope beyond measure in knowing God understands and is fully aware of our inability to achieve perfection on our own. This is the very reason He made a way for us to be restored. (Even though we deserved to be separated from Him because of Adam and Eve's fall—when they lost their connection to the Holy Spirit and in essence became a sophisticated self-centered animal, one dominated by self-preservation, self-agenda, and self-fulfillment.)

Read Genesis 2:16-17.

[16] And the Lord God commanded the man, saying, "You may surely eat of every tree of the garden, [17] but of the tree of the knowledge of good and evil you shall not eat, for in the day that you eat[a] of it you shall surely die."

Read Genesis 3:7-24.

[7] Then the eyes of both were opened, and they knew that they were naked. And they sewed fig leaves together and made themselves loincloths.
[8] And they heard the sound of the Lord God walking in the garden in the cool[a] of the day, and the man and his wife hid themselves from the presence of the Lord God among the trees of the garden. [9] But the Lord God called to the man and said to him, "Where are you?"[b] [10] And he said, "I heard the sound of you in the garden, and I was afraid, because I was naked, and I hid myself." [11] He

LESSON 3:
WHAT IS FORGIVENESS? (PART 1)

said, "Who told you that you were naked? Have you eaten of the tree of which I commanded you not to eat?" [12] The man said, "The woman whom you gave to be with me, she gave me fruit of the tree, and I ate." [13] Then the Lord God said to the woman, "What is this that you have done?" The woman said, "The serpent deceived me, and I ate."

[14] The Lord God said to the serpent,

"Because you have done this,
　cursed are you above all livestock
　and above all beasts of the field;
on your belly you shall go,
　and dust you shall eat
　all the days of your life.
[15] I will put enmity between you and the woman,
　and between your offspring[c] and her offspring;
he shall bruise your head,
　and you shall bruise his heel."
[16] To the woman he said,

"I will surely multiply your pain in childbearing;
　in pain you shall bring forth children.
Your desire shall be contrary to[d] your husband,
　but he shall rule over you."

[17] And to Adam he said,

"Because you have listened to the voice of your wife
　and have eaten of the tree
of which I commanded you,
　'You shall not eat of it,'
cursed is the ground because of you;
　in pain you shall eat of it all the days of your life;
[18] thorns and thistles it shall bring forth for you;
　and you shall eat the plants of the field.
[19] By the sweat of your face
　you shall eat bread,

LESSON 3:
WHAT IS FORGIVENESS? (PART 1)

> till you return to the ground,
>   for out of it you were taken;
> for you are dust,
>   and to dust you shall return."
>
> 20 The man called his wife's name Eve, because she was the mother of all living. [e] 21 And the Lord God made for Adam and for his wife garments of skins and clothed them.
>
> 22 Then the Lord God said, "Behold, the man has become like one of us in knowing good and evil. Now, lest he reach out his hand and take also of the tree of life and eat, and live forever—" 23 therefore the Lord God sent him out from the garden of Eden to work the ground from which he was taken. 24 He drove out the man, and at the east of the garden of Eden he placed the cherubim and a flaming sword that turned every way to guard the way to the tree of life.

At this point, man and woman deserved God's eternal wrath and anger. His holy creation wronged the Holy Creator. What were the consequences of this?

> **Read Psalm 103:9-10.**
>
> 9 He will not always chide,
>   nor will he keep his anger forever.
> 10 He does not deal with us according to our sins,
>   nor repay us according to our iniquities.

_____
_____
_____
_____
_____

LESSON 3:
WHAT IS FORGIVENESS? (PART 1)

> **Read Psalm 143:2.**
>
> ² Enter not into judgment with your servant,
>   for no one living is righteous before you.

_____
_____
_____
_____
_____

> **Read Psalm 130:3.**
>
> ³ If you, O Lord, should mark iniquities,
>   O Lord, who could stand?

_____
_____
_____
_____
_____

  Because God's nature is forgiveness, He did not eternally separate HIMSELF from HIS creation or demand that we achieve holiness on our own (this is the real requirement and the essence of the law), as this is something we never could achieve. Without His intervention, we would be separated eternally. Rather, He, based solely upon His nature of forgiveness, forgave us through the exchange of His life for our life as the remedy for reconciliation (more on reconciliation later). Thus, through His forgiveness (Himself), He died as the required sacrifice, the propitiation of Sin, the justification for Sin, and thus satisfied the requirement of holiness and perfect righteousness. He took the penalty of judgment for all His creation; and thus, at all times, offers all His creation the opportunity to be set free.

LESSON 3:
WHAT IS FORGIVENESS? (PART 1)

(Of course, this does require that we accept the offer of reconciliation, which we will explore this in more detail in the next lesson.)

Why do we deserve God's eternal wrath, and why (unless He offered an opportunity for forgiveness through His nature) would we would live eternally separated from Him? Think through the implication of this regarding our process of forgiveness and write your answers here.

_____
_____
_____
_____
_____
_____
_____
_____
_____
_____
_____
_____
_____
_____
_____
_____
_____
_____
_____
_____
_____
_____

LESSON 3:
WHAT IS FORGIVENESS? (PART 1)

LESSON 4:
WHAT IS FORGIVENESS? (PART 2)

Review your notes from Lesson 3, and restate the reason we deserve God's eternal wrath.

In the Old Testament, God's forgiveness was fulfilled through the sacrifice of a perfect lamb, once a year by the high priest on the Day of Atonement. It was the shedding of innocent blood in an exchange of the lamb's life for the lives of the people of Israel.

> **Read Leviticus 16-17 noting both the reasons we have access to God's forgiveness and the instructions for how Israel received atonement (forgiveness) for their iniquity once a year.**
>
> The Day of Atonement
> **16** The Lord spoke to Moses after the death of the two sons of Aaron, when they drew near before the Lord and died, [2] and the Lord said to Moses, "Tell Aaron your brother not to come at any time into the Holy Place inside the veil, before the mercy seat that is on the ark, so that he may not die. For I will appear in the cloud over the mercy seat. [3] But in this way Aaron shall come into the Holy Place: with a bull from the herd for a sin offering and a ram for a burnt offering. [4] He shall put on the holy linen coat and shall have the linen undergarment on his body, and he shall tie the linen sash around his waist, and wear the linen turban; these are the holy garments. He shall bathe his body in water and then put them on. [5] And he shall take from the congregation of the people of Israel two male goats for a sin offering, and one ram for a burnt offering.
>
> [6] "Aaron shall offer the bull as a sin offering for himself and shall make atonement for himself and for his house. [7] Then he shall take the two goats and set them before the Lord at the entrance of the tent of meeting. [8] And Aaron shall cast lots over the two goats, one lot for the Lord and the other lot for Azazel.[a] [9] And Aaron shall present the goat on which the lot fell for the Lord and use it as a sin offering, [10] but the goat

> "In the New Testament, God's forgiveness was fulfilled through the sacrifice (the exchange of Christ's life for our life) of The Perfect Lamb of God (the Father's only begotten Son, and our High Priest). It was once and for all, completed, finished."

LESSON 4:
WHAT IS FORGIVENESS? (PART 2)

on which the lot fell for Azazel shall be presented alive before the Lord to make atonement over it, that it may be sent away into the wilderness to Azazel.

[11] "Aaron shall present the bull as a sin offering for himself, and shall make atonement for himself and for his house. He shall kill the bull as a sin offering for himself. [12] And he shall take a censer full of coals of fire from the altar before the Lord, and two handfuls of sweet incense beaten small, and he shall bring it inside the veil [13] and put the incense on the fire before the Lord, that the cloud of the incense may cover the mercy seat that is over the testimony, so that he does not die. [14] And he shall take some of the blood of the bull and sprinkle it with his finger on the front of the mercy seat on the east side, and in front of the mercy seat he shall sprinkle some of the blood with his finger seven times.

[15] "Then he shall kill the goat of the sin offering that is for the people and bring its blood inside the veil and do with its blood as he did with the blood of the bull, sprinkling it over the mercy seat and in front of the mercy seat. [16] Thus he shall make atonement for the Holy Place, because of the uncleannesses of the people of Israel and because of their transgressions, all their sins. And so he shall do for the tent of meeting, which dwells with them in the midst of their uncleannesses. [17] No one may be in the tent of meeting from the time he enters to make atonement in the Holy Place until he comes out and has made atonement for himself and for his house and for all the assembly of Israel. [18] Then he shall go out to the altar that is before the Lord and make atonement for it, and shall take some of the blood of the bull and some of the blood of the goat, and put it on the horns of the altar all around. [19] And he shall sprinkle some of the blood on it with his finger seven times, and cleanse it and consecrate it from the uncleannesses of the people of Israel.

[20] "And when he has made an end of atoning for the Holy Place and the tent of meeting and the altar, he shall present the live goat. [21] And Aaron shall lay both his hands on the head of the live goat, and confess over it all the iniquities of the people of Israel, and all their transgressions, all their sins. And he shall put them on the head of the goat and send it away into the wilderness by the hand of a man who is in readiness. [22] The goat shall bear all their iniquities on itself to a remote area, and he shall let the goat go free in the wilderness.

LESSON 4:
WHAT IS FORGIVENESS? (PART 2)

23 "Then Aaron shall come into the tent of meeting and shall take off the linen garments that he put on when he went into the Holy Place and shall leave them there. 24 And he shall bathe his body in water in a holy place and put on his garments and come out and offer his burnt offering and the burnt offering of the people and make atonement for himself and for the people. 25 And the fat of the sin offering he shall burn on the altar. 26 And he who lets the goat go to Azazel shall wash his clothes and bathe his body in water, and afterward he may come into the camp. 27 And the bull for the sin offering and the goat for the sin offering, whose blood was brought in to make atonement in the Holy Place, shall be carried outside the camp. Their skin and their flesh and their dung shall be burned up with fire. 28 And he who burns them shall wash his clothes and bathe his body in water, and afterward he may come into the camp.

29 "And it shall be a statute to you forever that in the seventh month, on the tenth day of the month, you shall afflict yourselves[b] and shall do no work, either the native or the stranger who sojourns among you. 30 For on this day shall atonement be made for you to cleanse you. You shall be clean before the Lord from all your sins. 31 It is a Sabbath of solemn rest to you, and you shall afflict yourselves; it is a statute forever. 32 And the priest who is anointed and consecrated as priest in his father's place shall make atonement, wearing the holy linen garments. 33 He shall make atonement for the holy sanctuary, and he shall make atonement for the tent of meeting and for the altar, and he shall make atonement for the priests and for all the people of the assembly. 34 And this shall be a statute forever for you, that atonement may be made for the people of Israel once in the year because of all their sins." And Aaron[c] did as the Lord commanded Moses.

The Place of Sacrifice
17 And the Lord spoke to Moses, saying, 2 "Speak to Aaron and his sons and to all the people of Israel and say to them, this is the thing that the Lord has commanded. 3 If any one of the house of Israel kills an ox or a lamb or a goat in the camp, or kills it outside the camp, 4 and does not bring it to the entrance of the tent of meeting to offer it as a gift to the Lord in front of the tabernacle of the Lord, bloodguilt shall be imputed to that man. He has shed blood, and that man shall be cut off from among his people. 5 This is to the end that the people of Israel may bring their sacrifices that they sacrifice in the open field, that they may bring them to the Lord, to the priest at the entrance of the tent of meeting, and sacrifice them as sacrifices of peace offerings to the Lord. 6 And the priest

LESSON 4:
WHAT IS FORGIVENESS? (PART 2)

shall throw the blood on the altar of the Lord at the entrance of the tent of meeting and burn the fat for a pleasing aroma to the Lord. ⁷ So they shall no more sacrifice their sacrifices to goat demons, after whom they whore. This shall be a statute forever for them throughout their generations.

⁸ "And you shall say to them, any one of the house of Israel, or of the strangers who sojourn among them, who offers a burnt offering or sacrifice ⁹ and does not bring it to the entrance of the tent of meeting to offer it to the Lord, that man shall be cut off from his people.

Laws Against Eating Blood
¹⁰ "If any one of the house of Israel or of the strangers who sojourn among them eats any blood, I will set my face against that person who eats blood and will cut him off from among his people. ¹¹ For the life of the flesh is in the blood, and I have given it for you on the altar to make atonement for your souls, for it is the blood that makes atonement by the life.¹² Therefore I have said to the people of Israel, no person among you shall eat blood, neither shall any stranger who sojourns among you eat blood.

¹³ "Any one also of the people of Israel, or of the strangers who sojourn among them, who takes in hunting any beast or bird that may be eaten shall pour out its blood and cover it with earth. ¹⁴ For the life of every creature[d] is its blood: its blood is its life.[e] Therefore I have said to the people of Israel, You shall not eat the blood of any creature, for the life of every creature is its blood. Whoever eats it shall be cut off. ¹⁵ And every person who eats what dies of itself or what is torn by beasts, whether he is a native or a sojourner, shall wash his clothes and bathe himself in water and be unclean until the evening; then he shall be clean. ¹⁶ But if he does not wash them or bathe his flesh, he shall bear his iniquity."

_____
_____
_____
_____

LESSON 4:
WHAT IS FORGIVENESS? (PART 2)

Though this provided atonement and forgiveness for one year, it was not permanent. The high priest who fulfilled the sacrifice in the Holy of Holies through the shedding of blood, could not sit down but only stand to symbolize that the sacrifice was not permanent.

In the New Testament, God's forgiveness was fulfilled through the sacrifice (the exchange of Christ's life for our life) of The Perfect Lamb of God (the Father's only begotten Son, and our High Priest). It was once and for all, completed, finished. It was forgiveness fulfilled for all, for all time. Read through these verses and identify what Christ has done/completed on our behalf to "forgive" us?

> **Read Romans 3:21-26.**
>
> The Righteousness of God Through Faith
> 21 But now the righteousness of God has been manifested apart from the law, although the Law and the Prophets bear witness to it— 22 the righteousness of God through faith in Jesus Christ for all who believe. For there is no distinction: 23 for all have sinned and fall short of the glory of God, 24 and are justified by his grace as a gift, through the redemption that is in Christ Jesus, 25 whom God put forward as a propitiation by his blood, to be received by faith. This was to show God's righteousness, because in his divine forbearance he had passed over former sins. 26 It was to show his righteousness at the present time, so that he might be just and the justifier of the one who has faith in Jesus.

_____
_____
_____
_____
_____

> **Read Ephesians 1:7-12.**
>
> 7 In him we have redemption through his blood, the forgiveness of our trespasses, according to the riches of his grace, 8 which he lavished upon us, in

LESSON 4:
WHAT IS FORGIVENESS? (PART 2)

> all wisdom and insight ⁹ making known[a] to us the mystery of his will, according to his purpose, which he set forth in Christ¹⁰ as a plan for the fullness of time, to unite all things in him, things in heaven and things on earth.
>
> ¹¹ In him we have obtained an inheritance, having been predestined according to the purpose of him who works all things according to the counsel of his will, ¹² so that we who were the first to hope in Christ might be to the praise of his glory.

_____
_____
_____
_____
_____

> **Read Hebrews 9:1-10:18.**
>
> The Earthly Holy Place
> **9** Now even the first covenant had regulations for worship and an earthly place of holiness.² For a tent[a] was prepared, the first section, in which were the lampstand and the table and the bread of the Presence.[b] It is called the Holy Place. ³ Behind the second curtain was a second section[c] called the Most Holy Place, ⁴ having the golden altar of incense and the ark of the covenant covered on all sides with gold, in which was a golden urn holding the manna, and Aaron's staff that budded, and the tablets of the covenant. ⁵ Above it were the cherubim of glory overshadowing the mercy seat. Of these things we cannot now speak in detail.
>
> ⁶ These preparations having thus been made, the priests go regularly into the first section, performing their ritual duties, ⁷ but into the second only the high priest goes, and he but once a year, and not without taking blood, which he offers for himself and for the unintentional sins of the people. ⁸ By this the Holy Spirit indicates that the way into the holy places is not yet opened as long as the first section is still standing ⁹ (which is symbolic for the present age).

LESSON 4:
WHAT IS FORGIVENESS? (PART 2)

[d]According to this arrangement, gifts and sacrifices are offered that cannot perfect the conscience of the worshiper, 10 but deal only with food and drink and various washings, regulations for the body imposed until the time of reformation.

Redemption Through the Blood of Christ
11 But when Christ appeared as a high priest of the good things that have come,[e] then through the greater and more perfect tent (not made with hands, that is, not of this creation) 12 he entered once for all into the holy places, not by means of the blood of goats and calves but by means of his own blood, thus securing an eternal redemption. 13 For if the blood of goats and bulls, and the sprinkling of defiled persons with the ashes of a heifer, sanctify[f] for the purification of the flesh, 14 how much more will the blood of Christ, who through the eternal Spirit offered himself without blemish to God, purify our[g] conscience from dead works to serve the living God.

15 Therefore he is the mediator of a new covenant, so that those who are called may receive the promised eternal inheritance, since a death has occurred that redeems them from the transgressions committed under the first covenant. [h] 16 For where a will is involved, the death of the one who made it must be established. 17 For a will takes effect only at death, since it is not in force as long as the one who made it is alive. 18 Therefore not even the first covenant was inaugurated without blood. 19 For when every commandment of the law had been declared by Moses to all the people, he took the blood of calves and goats, with water and scarlet wool and hyssop, and sprinkled both the book itself and all the people, 20 saying, "This is the blood of the covenant that God commanded for you." 21 And in the same way he sprinkled with the blood both the tent and all the vessels used in worship. 22 Indeed, under the law almost everything is purified with blood, and without the shedding of blood there is no forgiveness of sins.

23 Thus it was necessary for the copies of the heavenly things to be purified with these rites, but the heavenly things themselves with better sacrifices than these. 24 For Christ has entered, not into holy places made with hands, which are copies of the true things, but into heaven itself, now to appear in the presence of God on our behalf. 25 Nor was it to offer himself repeatedly, as the high priest enters the holy places every year with blood not his own, 26 for then he would have had to suffer repeatedly since the foundation of the world. But as

LESSON 4:
WHAT IS FORGIVENESS? (PART 2)

it is, he has appeared once for all at the end of the ages to put away sin by the sacrifice of himself. ²⁷ And just as it is appointed for man to die once, and after that comes judgment,²⁸ so Christ, having been offered once to bear the sins of many, will appear a second time, not to deal with sin but to save those who are eagerly waiting for him.

Christ's Sacrifice Once for All
10 For since the law has but a shadow of the good things to come instead of the true form of these realities, it can never, by the same sacrifices that are continually offered every year, make perfect those who draw near. ² Otherwise, would they not have ceased to be offered, since the worshipers, having once been cleansed, would no longer have any consciousness of sins? ³ But in these sacrifices there is a reminder of sins every year. ⁴ For it is impossible for the blood of bulls and goats to take away sins.

⁵ Consequently, when Christ[i] came into the world, he said,

"Sacrifices and offerings you have not desired,
   but a body have you prepared for me;
⁶ in burnt offerings and sin offerings
   you have taken no pleasure.
⁷ Then I said, 'Behold, I have come to do your will, O God,
   as it is written of me in the scroll of the book.'"

⁸ When he said above, "You have neither desired nor taken pleasure in sacrifices and offerings and burnt offerings and sin offerings" (these are offered according to the law), ⁹ then he added, "Behold, I have come to do your will." He does away with the first in order to establish the second. ¹⁰ And by that will we have been sanctified through the offering of the body of Jesus Christ once for all.

¹¹ And every priest stands daily at his service, offering repeatedly the same sacrifices, which can never take away sins. ¹² But when Christ[j] had offered for all time a single sacrifice for sins, he sat down at the right hand of God, ¹³ waiting from that time until his enemies should be made a footstool for his feet. ¹⁴ For by a single offering he has perfected for all time those who are being sanctified.

LESSON 4:
WHAT IS FORGIVENESS? (PART 2)

> ¹⁵ And the Holy Spirit also bears witness to us; for after saying,
>
> ¹⁶ "This is the covenant that I will make with them
>   after those days, declares the Lord:
> I will put my laws on their hearts,
>   and write them on their minds,"
>
> ¹⁷ then he adds,
>
> "I will remember their sins and their lawless deeds no more."
>
> ¹⁸ Where there is forgiveness of these, there is no longer any offering for sin.

_____
_____
_____
_____

> **Read 1 John 4:7-11.**
>
> God Is Love
>
> ⁷ Beloved, let us love one another, for love is from God, and whoever loves has been born of God and knows God. ⁸ Anyone who does not love does not know God, because God is love. ⁹ In this the love of God was made manifest among us, that God sent his only Son into the world, so that we might live through him. ¹⁰ In this is love, not that we have loved God but that he loved us and sent his Son to be the propitiation for our sins. ¹¹ Beloved, if God so loved us, we also ought to love one another.

_____
_____
_____
_____
_____

LESSON 4:
WHAT IS FORGIVENESS? (PART 2)

What is the hope amidst a seemingly hopeless situation? The New Testament tells of God's perfect lamb, Jesus, "God with Us" dying on our behalf. Through God's forgiving nature, Christ exchanged His own life for ours as the remedy for reconciliation and forgave us our sin. The Father's only begotten Son and our High Priest died, sacrificed Himself, in order to fulfill the law to restore communion. He died as the propitiation (appeasement or placation) of our sin; He died as a justification of (setting us free from) sin; His perfect righteousness and holiness is given to us in exchange. He died to take the penalty of judgment for all His creation and, in turn, offers that same creation the opportunity to be free. Jesus died once for all mankind, and the full appeasement of sin has been completed, it has been finished. Forgiveness has been fulfilled for all people, for all time.

Mankind was separated from God because of sin. Upon entering the Garden of Eden, sin killed man's spirit, and the intimate communion once shared between God and man and woman was irrevocably broken. Sin, evil, and a self-satisfying will have no fellowship or association with the Holy God. Nevertheless, love and forgiveness prevailed. God Himself provided the remedy needed to satisfy His holy demands to restore the broken relationship. God became man in Jesus, dwelt among mankind, and then died for humanity's sin. If God had to implement forgiveness based merely on when and if we deserve it, God never would have offered it. Again, forgiveness from God has nothing to do with what we deserve—it is based solely on God's nature, who He IS. God forgives. To anyone who asks, God passes over our sins, remembers them no more, and replaces our sin with a cloak of His own righteousness.

Such a difficult concept is sometimes more easily understood through fiction. If you have read the *Chronicles of Narnia*, then you may remember Aslan. He was the lion who in *The Magician's Nephew* sung the world of Narnia into existence. Everything from the stars to the grass, Aslan sung it into existence. The story continues in *The Lion, the Witch, and the Wardrobe* where the White Witch deceives Edmund, and his traitorous actions require him to die. However, the Creator of Narnia, Aslan, dies in Edmund's place: the horrible and torturous death of a sinless one on behalf of a sinner deserving death. Such is the story of Christ in reality. A sinless one died on behalf of sinners. The Creator dying on behalf of the creation.

But Aslan did not remain dead. He broke the stone table and rose from the dead victorious. Neither did Jesus remain dead, or we would have no hope. In Christ's death, He took upon Himself the sin of the world and rose from the dead only a few days later.

Upon His satisfying the requirements of taking upon Himself the judgment for sin through His death on the cross, He was resurrected into the new, superabundant life eternal. Read through these verses and identify what His resurrection then has provided to us:

LESSON 4:
WHAT IS FORGIVENESS? (PART 2)

Read John 11:17-27.

I Am the Resurrection and the Life

17 Now when Jesus came, he found that Lazarus had already been in the tomb four days. 18 Bethany was near Jerusalem, about two miles[a] off, 19 and many of the Jews had come to Martha and Mary to console them concerning their brother. 20 So when Martha heard that Jesus was coming, she went and met him, but Mary remained seated in the house. 21 Martha said to Jesus, "Lord, if you had been here, my brother would not have died. 22 But even now I know that whatever you ask from God, God will give you." 23 Jesus said to her, "Your brother will rise again." 24 Martha said to him, "I know that he will rise again in the resurrection on the last day." 25 Jesus said to her, "I am the resurrection and the life.[b] Whoever believes in me, though he die, yet shall he live, 26 and everyone who lives and believes in me shall never die. Do you believe this?" 27 She said to him, "Yes, Lord; I believe that you are the Christ, the Son of God, who is coming into the world."

_____
_____
_____
_____

Read John 14:15-26.

Jesus Promises the Holy Spirit

15 "If you love me, you will keep my commandments. 16 And I will ask the Father, and he will give you another Helper,[a] to be with you forever, 17 even the Spirit of truth, whom the world cannot receive, because it neither sees him nor knows him. You know him, for he dwells with you and will be[b] in you.

18 "I will not leave you as orphans; I will come to you. 19 Yet a little while and the world will see me no more, but you will see me. Because I live, you also will live. 20 In that day you will know that I am in my Father, and you in me,

LESSON 4:
WHAT IS FORGIVENESS? (PART 2)

and I in you. ²¹ Whoever has my commandments and keeps them, he it is who loves me. And he who loves me will be loved by my Father, and I will love him and manifest myself to him." ²² Judas (not Iscariot) said to him, "Lord, how is it that you will manifest yourself to us, and not to the world?" ²³ Jesus answered him, "If anyone loves me, he will keep my word, and my Father will love him, and we will come to him and make our home with him. ²⁴ Whoever does not love me does not keep my words. And the word that you hear is not mine but the Father's who sent me.

²⁵ "These things I have spoken to you while I am still with you. ²⁶ But the Helper, the Holy Spirit, whom the Father will send in my name, he will teach you all things and bring to your remembrance all that I have said to you.

_____
_____
_____
_____
_____

Read John 10:10.

¹⁰ The thief comes only to steal and kill and destroy. I came that they may have life and have it abundantly.

_____
_____
_____
_____
_____

Once He satisfied God the Father's requirement for sin upon Himself, He rose from the grave victorious and was resurrected into an eternal new life, even more abundant than before, putting to death the law (what the stone table represents). Jesus, after all, was and is the resurrection and the life.

LESSON 4:
WHAT IS FORGIVENESS? (PART 2)

It is a paradox. Through His death, He attained life. He exchanged His life for mine, for yours, for all of mankind's. When we die to self, we live in the Spirit. Only in God's economy do equations work out like this. Everything God did through sending His Son, everything His Son, Jesus, did was due to the nature of forgiveness inherent within the Almighty. Because of this forgiveness, and only because of it, do we have the opportunity to once again be restored to our former, exceptional place in life. Our extraordinary identity can be regained, and then some. We can exercise our exceptional authority and take ground against the kingdom of the world, dominated by the work of the enemy. We can once again enjoy exceptional work, every day looking forward to our occupation. We can expect that our marriages will become exceptional in all aspects. We can trust God for exceptional provision. That beautiful, exceptional communion with God, once lost, can be restored and surpass what Adam had in the beginning. Praise God and thank him for washing your sin away! Receive the reconciliation to the Father through the Son. Embrace the cross and be forever changed.

Thus, through death, He attained life, mankind's life that He exchanged of His life. This all was due to His nature of forgiveness. Only as a result of this forgiveness do we have the opportunity to once again be restored to our intended place—holy, perfect righteousness—Spiritual communion with God. But to actually experience this we must accept His offer of reconciliation, which, through belief, also exchanges our life for His life. We must admit our eternal is separation due to sin, we must die to self, and agree to receive His life in us (i.e., born again with the Holy Spirit as is written in John 3:3-5).

There is a critical truth about all this regarding our ability to forgive others: If God operated based solely upon what is deserved, we would all experience eternal separation from God with no hope of ever again having a relationship with Him. The only reason we have the possibility of reconciliation is His nature of forgiveness. So, forgiveness is only available for us to receive and give away because of His nature. We love because He first loved us. We forgive because He first forgave us. This is important as we explore what this means in our everyday life. Forgiveness is not letting someone off the hook because they satisfied some requirement of ours. Forgiveness is God's nature in us, operating toward another person who deserves our wrath and anger. Forgiveness, then, is actually not between me and another person, but is between me and God, His Spirit in us, His nature in us.

LESSON 4:
WHAT IS FORGIVENESS? (PART 2)

So, in other words:

If His level of forgiveness were based upon what we deserve, then what would happen to us eternally?

_____
_____
_____
_____
_____

(eternal un-forgiveness and separation)

If His level of forgiveness were based upon us doing better and trying harder (good works), then what would happen to us eternally?

_____
_____
_____
_____
_____

(eternal un-forgiveness and separation)

If His level of forgiveness were based upon us asking for a reprieve from a kind and generous judge, then what would happen to us?

_____
_____
_____
_____
_____

(eternal un-forgiveness and separation).

LESSON 4:
WHAT IS FORGIVENESS? (PART 2)

IT IS NOT BASED UPON OUR RESPONSE, BUT UPON HIS NATURE. HE IS FORGIVENESS! AND WITHOUT THIS FORGIVENESS, THERE IS NO POSSIBILITY OF RECONCILIATION.

So, through His death and now living in the Resurrection, has Christ forgiven everyone? _____ *(Yes! Once and for all, it is completed, finished.)*

Does He have any difficulty or struggle in extending forgiveness to anyone? _____*(No! It is already done, completed, finished.)*

Does someone have to fix all their mistakes and act perfectly? _____ *(No)*

Does someone have to live out a "second class," mediocre life and only experience partial forgiveness by:

Staying in guilt? Grief? _____ *(No)*

Being unable to correct things? _____ *(No)*

Being reminded of failures? _____ *(No)*

An inability to regain the best? _____ *(No)*

Does someone have to wait until they perform? _____ *(No)*

How fast can we experience God's forgiveness toward us?

> **Read 1 John 1:9.**
>
> ⁹ If we confess our sins, he is faithful and just to forgive us our sins and to cleanse us from all unrighteousness.

_____
_____
_____
_____
_____

LESSON 4:
WHAT IS FORGIVENESS? (PART 2)

(Instantaneous; nanosecond)

Why?

_____
_____
_____
_____
_____

(Not based upon what we do, but on His nature and what He has already done!)

So, He is forgiveness and offers forgiveness endlessly to all His human creation—every moment, all the time, every time.

When we embrace the cross and the Lamb who died upon the cross, when we receive forgiveness and reconciliation from the Father, we are forever changed. Indeed, the old has gone, and the new has come. And yet, there is a great and joyful responsibility given to us as we interact with our world as these new creations. We are called to forgive others as God has forgiven us. Is this difficult to do? No, it is impossible to do without the Spirit's assistance, doing it in and through us!

To break things down:

- If God forgave based upon what we deserve, then eternal un-forgiveness and separation would necessarily ensue.

- If God's forgiveness were dependent upon us doing better, trying harder, attempting good works, then eternal un-forgiveness and separation would be inevitable.

- If God based His forgiveness upon us asking for a pardon as from a kind and generous judge, then eternal un-forgiveness and separation would be the sentence.

We must fully understand and internalize the truth that forgiveness has nothing, absolutely nothing, to do with our response. Divine forgiveness rests fully upon God's nature: He is forgiveness. Without this nature, without this forgiveness, there is no possibility of reconciliation to the Father whatsoever. Through Christ's death and subsequent glorious resurrection, everyone has already been forgiven. He died once for all, and the work demanded of Christ is indeed finished,

LESSON 4:
WHAT IS FORGIVENESS? (PART 2)

completed. Because the work has already been done, since the guilt and wages of sin have been forever atoned for, Jesus has absolutely no difficulty nor struggle in extending forgiveness to anyone, even you. It matters not your past, your present circumstances, your gender, your race, or your creed. Jesus offers this wonderful gift to all of mankind. Put your mind at ease, friend. You are free to run to Jesus and accept this beautiful gift just as you are, right now! You are not required to fix all of your mistakes or get all of your proverbial ducks in a row before being acceptable to Him. In fact, it is impossible to do so.

> "God's forgiveness is full and complete. There are no 'second class citizens' in the Kingdom."

The forgiveness offered to you accepts you just as you are and by One who loves you just as you are and more than you could comprehend. There is no partiality in God's family, either. God's forgiveness is full and complete. There are no "second class citizens" in the Kingdom. He extends forgiveness and reconciliation to you even if you are guilty, even if you are grieving, even if you are not able to correct your mistakes, or are incapable of forgetting your past failures.

You do not have to perform in order for Him to notice you or to earn your way in any shape or form. Remember, this gift is based not upon our ability to do the right things or obey God's law, it is a gift freely bestowed upon those who deserve it not.

Based upon these words, you might be asking yourself how quickly can you experience God's forgiveness? God's Word tells us that it is instantaneous.

How is this possible? Again, it is not based upon what we do, but upon His nature and what He has already done. The Almighty God is, by nature, forgiving and offers forgiveness endlessly to all His human creation—every moment, all the time, every time.

If we understand that forgiveness is neither a human quality nor something that we actually "do," but rather it is God Himself and something we receive, we can then begin to comprehend we are able to forgive everyone 100 percent of the time. This is only possible because forgiveness is not actually between me and another person, but rather between me and God, who has already forgiven everyone. The work of forgiveness has already been completed, and because His forgiveness is complete and present, this forgiveness can flow through us to others who have wronged us. This is accomplished on the same basis that He forgave us: God's nature. Not based on what we deserve or what others deserve from us but based on His own nature and the work He completed on the cross.

Be further encouraged by stories from Scripture. God's Word gives us example after example of those who deserved God's wrath, but instead experienced God's forgiveness:

LESSON 4:
WHAT IS FORGIVENESS? (PART 2)

- Noah was known as a drunk, but God used him mightily.

- Abraham lied about who his wife really was, but God gave him the covenant.

- Isaac lied and stole his brother's inheritance, but God changed his name to Israel.

- Moses disobeyed God and had a speech impediment, but he led the Israelites out of Egypt.

- David did his share of sinning but was still known as a man after God's own heart.

- Peter denied Jesus and had a temper but led thousands to the Lord.

- Paul originally killed Christians, but God used him mightily to reach the Gentiles.

These are but a few of the imperfect humans who did things that deserved God's wrath, but because of God's nature, received His forgiveness and were able to live an intimate life of joy with the Father.

Now, since God's nature is forgiveness, what about all the people in Scripture who did not enjoy His forgiveness? How is this possible even though we have already said all have been forgiven? How do these two truths reconcile? It all has to do with reconciliation. Reconciliation is not forgiveness and forgiveness is not reconciliation. It takes two parties to receive forgiveness and to be reconciled. God has no problem with forgiveness—He has forgiven all, but not all have responded to the truth and gift offered to them. Because of this, they remain un-reconciled to God. First of all, how have you responded to God's gift of forgiveness? Have you received it personally? If so, then you are fully reconciled to God—rejoice! Since it is our call to forgive others, revisit that list of individuals you complied at the beginning of the book. Have you come to the point of forgiving some of them? Any of them? All of them? Forgiveness is a choice based upon God's nature and based upon His work already done in you. You may not feel like forgiving these people, but I encourage you to forgive them in spite of your feelings. Make the choice, now, to forgive based upon the work of Christ, based upon Christ living within you, and let all that bitterness and anger and guilt go. Take as long as you

LESSON 4:
WHAT IS FORGIVENESS? (PART 2)

need to, but do not neglect this vital step to living in the fullness and abundance of the Kingdom.

Write out what you understand as to why God has forgiven us and the key truths about this forgiveness. What do these mean for you personally and your ability to forgive others?

_____
_____
_____
_____
_____
_____
_____
_____
_____
_____
_____
_____
_____
_____
_____
_____
_____
_____
_____
_____
_____
_____
_____
_____
_____

LESSON 4:
WHAT IS FORGIVENESS? (PART 2)

LESSON 5:
WHAT IS RECONCILIATION? (PART 1)

Since God is forgiveness, since it is His nature, and He has finished the work of forgiveness toward us who deserve His wrath and un-forgiveness, the key question is this: Do all people automatically experience this forgiveness? No.

God is forgiving; forgiveness is at the core of His nature. The work done on the cross, once and for all, was and is still very powerful. That work alone is what gives separated and estranged humanity hope of a relationship with a holy and wholly separate and unique God. But even though God has already forgiven all of humanity because of the cross and has no hesitation about to whom He offers it, such forgiveness does not automatically translate into reconciliation. Why doesn't all of humanity experience God's forgiveness? Because forgiveness can only be experienced through true reconciliation. Think about it. When there is a conflict between two people or groups of people, forgiveness is offered by one side because their desire is to once more have a relationship with the other. Each side must process through the offense and hurt done to get to point where each is able to move on, to let go of their anger and frustration. Both parties' expectations for continuing in relationship must be satisfied. Such actions and resolved tension lead to a deeper relationship, a deeper trust, and respect is experienced. Without forgiveness, a relationship cannot exist. Without trust, no relationship can stand.

Consider this:
Do you experience this forgiveness automatically because of His nature, and thus all experience it? _____ *(No)*

Remember, forgiveness is only experienced by reconciliation. By definition, reconciliation is between two parties. How?

_____
_____
_____
_____
_____

(Each party must process truth to a resolution satisfactory to both parties.)

> "God is forgiving; forgiveness is at the core of His nature. The work done on the cross, once and for all, was and is still very powerful."

LESSON 5:
WHAT IS RECONCILIATION? (PART 1)

What is the truth that satisfies Christ's offer of forgiveness to be reconciled to Him?

- God is holy and requires holiness and perfect righteousness.

- He cannot touch nor associate with un-holiness and un-righteousness.

- All have fallen short of this requirement and thus deserve His wrath and eternal separation. We stand condemned.

- He has performed the necessary exchange of His life through His death for our life—satisfying the requirement of holiness and perfect righteousness.

- If we believe this in our heart (soul) to be true, we pass from condemnation to life—reconciled; if we do not believe, we remain condemned, separated from God—not reconciled.

Read these verses, and write the truths about our position before God and the truth of reconciliation:

Read John 3:15-18.

For God So Loved the World
[16] "For God so loved the world,[b] that he gave his only Son, that whoever believes in him should not perish but have eternal life. [17] For God did not send his Son into the world to condemn the world, but in order that the world might be saved through him. [18] Whoever believes in him is not condemned, but whoever does not believe is condemned already, because he has not believed in the name of the only Son of God.

_____
_____
_____
_____
_____

LESSON 5:
WHAT IS RECONCILIATION? (PART 1)

> **Read John 5:24.**
>
> ²⁴ Truly, truly, I say to you, whoever hears my word and believes him who sent me has eternal life. He does not come into judgment, but has passed from death to life.

_____
_____
_____
_____
_____

> **Read Colossians 1:9-23.**
>
> ⁹ And so, from the day we heard, we have not ceased to pray for you, asking that you may be filled with the knowledge of his will in all spiritual wisdom and understanding, ¹⁰ so as to walk in a manner worthy of the Lord, fully pleasing to him: bearing fruit in every good work and increasing in the knowledge of God; ¹¹ being strengthened with all power, according to his glorious might, for all endurance and patience with joy; ¹² giving thanks[a] to the Father, who has qualified you[b] to share in the inheritance of the saints in light. ¹³ He has delivered us from the domain of darkness and transferred us to the kingdom of his beloved Son, ¹⁴ in whom we have redemption, the forgiveness of sins.
>
> The Preeminence of Christ
> ¹⁵ He is the image of the invisible God, the firstborn of all creation. ¹⁶ For by[c] him all things were created, in heaven and on earth, visible and invisible, whether thrones or dominions or rulers or authorities—all things were created through him and for him. ¹⁷ And he is before all things, and in him all things hold together. ¹⁸ And he is the head of the body, the church. He is the beginning, the firstborn from the dead, that in everything he might be preeminent. ¹⁹ For in him all the fullness of God was pleased to dwell, ²⁰ and through him to reconcile to himself all things, whether on earth or in heaven, making peace by the blood of his cross.

LESSON 5:
WHAT IS RECONCILIATION? (PART 1)

> ²¹ And you, who once were alienated and hostile in mind, doing evil deeds, ²² he has now reconciled in his body of flesh by his death, in order to present you holy and blameless and above reproach before him, ²³ if indeed you continue in the faith, stable and steadfast, not shifting from the hope of the gospel that you heard, which has been proclaimed in all creation[d] under heaven, and of which I, Paul, became a minister.

_____
_____
_____
_____
_____

    What is the truth that satisfies Christ's offer of forgiveness to be reconciled to Him? While this is a good question, to answer we must re-visit who God is and look again at His nature. God is holy. God is "wholly other" than his creation, and since this is true we must understand He requires holiness and perfect righteousness of all who come into His presence. Because of His holiness, He neither can come in contact nor associate with un-holiness and un-righteousness—in essence, ungodliness. It is no surprise that we cannot attain to such a high expectation. Scripture says all men and women have fallen short of this requirement, thusly deserving of His wrath and unforgiveness. We stand condemned already; we stand eternally separated already; we stand hopeless already…but there is hope. Christ has already performed the necessary requirements satisfying God's demands of holiness and righteousness. He offers His perfect life for our imperfect one, His horrible death in exchange for our impending death, His death leads to our life. In order to receive, we have to believe this beautiful gift offered to us is true in the deepest part of ourselves, our heart—our soul. When this happens, our condemnation is substituted for life abundant and we are reconciled to God forever. If we do not believe, we remain condemned, we remain separated from God, we remain hopeless, and reconciliation cannot be attained.

Does Christ alter any of this truth to be reconciled to His created humans?
_____ *(No)*

LESSON 5:
WHAT IS RECONCILIATION? (PART 1)

Read these verses and write down the truth regarding the way to reconciliation to God:

> **Read John 14:6.**
>
> ⁶ Jesus said to him, "I am the way, and the truth, and the life. No one comes to the Father except through me.

_____
_____
_____
_____
_____

> **Read John 3:36.**
>
> ³⁶ Whoever believes in the Son has eternal life; whoever does not obey the Son shall not see life, but the wrath of God remains on him.

_____
_____
_____
_____
_____

> **Read 1 John 5:12.**
>
> ¹² Whoever has the Son has life; whoever does not have the Son of God does not have life.

LESSON 5:
WHAT IS RECONCILIATION? (PART 1)

_____
_____
_____
_____
_____

This begs the question: Does Christ alter any of this truth in order to be reconciled to humanity? Absolutely not! As forgiving and desirous as Christ is in order to be reconciled to His creation, He in no way alters the truth set forth in His Word. Christ is, always has been, and always will be, the only way to be reconciled with God.

Does Christ let us NOT be reconciled and eternally separated from Him, even though He has finished the work of forgiveness? _____ *(Yes)*

Why?
_____
_____
_____
_____
_____

What do these verses say about what Truth/Word will judge us? What does this mean about how we live and the truth about reconciliation?

Read Hebrews 4:11-13.

¹¹ Let us therefore strive to enter that rest, so that no one may fall by the same sort of disobedience. ¹² For the word of God is living and active, sharper than any two-edged sword, piercing to the division of soul and of spirit, of joints and of marrow, and discerning the thoughts and intentions of the heart. ¹³ And no creature is hidden from his sight, but all are naked and exposed to the eyes of him to whom we must give account.

LESSON 5:
WHAT IS RECONCILIATION? (PART 1)

Read John 12:42-50.

⁴² Nevertheless, many even of the authorities believed in him, but for fear of the Pharisees they did not confess it, so that they would not be put out of the synagogue; ⁴³ for they loved the glory that comes from man more than the glory that comes from God.

Jesus Came to Save the World
⁴⁴ And Jesus cried out and said, "Whoever believes in me, believes not in me but in him who sent me. ⁴⁵ And whoever sees me sees him who sent me. ⁴⁶ I have come into the world as light, so that whoever believes in me may not remain in darkness. ⁴⁷ If anyone hears my words and does not keep them, I do not judge him; for I did not come to judge the world but to save the world. ⁴⁸ The one who rejects me and does not receive my words has a judge; the word that I have spoken will judge him on the last day. ⁴⁹ For I have not spoken on my own authority, but the Father who sent me has himself given me a commandment—what to say and what to speak. ⁵⁰ And I know that his commandment is eternal life. What I say, therefore, I say as the Father has told me."

It must be processed by the other party to be reconciled and receive the benefits of forgiveness.

LESSON 5:
WHAT IS RECONCILIATION? (PART 1)

Amidst all of the beauty and hope and relief experienced in the realization of forgiveness offered, there is a hard truth to accept and know. In order to maintain His holiness and perfection, Christ will allow His creation, humanity, not to be reconciled and remain eternally separated from God, even though the work of forgiveness has been finished. This is a tough concept to comprehend and prevents many from accepting such a beautiful gift. Many people cannot accept a loving and forgiving God who does not automatically forgive all of His creation. However, truth must be maintained in order for it to remain truth. God's truth must be able to stand on its own, independently, and cannot change in order for God to remain true to His nature of being completely holy and righteous. Where would we be if God changed His mind or requirements for appeasing His wrath on a case-by-case basis? We would be dealing with a being much like ourselves, not a God who is wholly other and different from His creation. We must first be relegated to the fact that humanity is, by nature, unrighteous and unholy and permanently separated from God who is completely righteous and holy. The conundrum presented between separated humanity and God's desire to reconcile has but one solution. Christ is the only remedy, the only way to bridge that separation, and the only part we play is to believe and receive the work Christ has already accomplished on the cross on our behalf. Christ Himself does not alter the truth He died for or lived for. Through His compassion, Christ allows reconciliation but still stands firmly on the redemptive work done through His death, burial, and resurrection. It is this work which allows Him to freely offer the opportunity for reconciliation to all of mankind.

So, the gift of forgiveness must be believed in and then fully received and accepted in order for reconciliation and all of its benefits to be experienced. Again, the truth stands on its own. Christ has a heart and compassion for all to be reconciled to Him, just like 2 Peter 3:9 says:

> 9 The Lord is not slow to fulfill his promise as some count slowness, but is patient toward you,[a] not wishing that any should perish, but that all should reach repentance.

Does this mean Christ lets us NOT be reconciled to God and therefore be eternally separated from Him—even though He has finished the work of forgiveness? Yes. Remember, reconciliation requires truth to be accepted—and Christ does not alter the truth in order that a person may accept a partial element of truth to achieve reconciliation. What is this truth? The unalterable truth found in Christ. Although He has completely forgiven all, once and for all, and continually

LESSON 5:
WHAT IS RECONCILIATION? (PART 1)

offers reconciliation to all, not all will be reconciled because of their unwillingness to receive it, process through it, and believe upon it. As a result, those who do not process the truth of their own sinfulness, believe upon and in Christ's redemptive work, and receive His forgiveness will spend eternity un-reconciled and will live eternally separated in hell from the Father, Son, and Holy Spirit.

Who are the people you know who are not reconciled to the Father? Who among your friends and family members have yet to believe and receive the unconditional love and forgiveness offered by Christ? With such a vitally important question hanging in the balance, prayerfully consider how to ask this question to your friends and family. Ask for wisdom and boldness as you embark on sharing with others how the cross of Christ has changed you. Forgiveness and reconciliation to God is amazingly good news, so share it joyfully and see where God takes you on your journey.

As believers, children of God, what does this mean to us?

If we have accepted Christ as our savior, can we be separated from Him again—not experiencing this fellowship? _____

Eternally? _____ *(No)*

What do these verses say about our eternal position once we have accepted Christ as our Lord and Savior?

> **Read John 5:24.**
>
> ²⁴ Truly, truly, I say to you, whoever hears my word and believes him who sent me has eternal life. He does not come into judgment, but has passed from death to life.

_____

_____

_____

_____

LESSON 5:
WHAT IS RECONCILIATION? (PART 1)

> **Read 1 John 5:11-12.**
>
> [11] And this is the testimony, that God gave us eternal life, and this life is in his Son. [12] Whoever has the Son has life; whoever does not have the Son of God does not have life.

_____
_____
_____
_____
_____

What about those of us who have been reconciled, through accepting and believing His truth? This topic of being disconnected and estranged comes into the believer's mind from time to time, and some of those times we have questions about forgiveness and reconciliation. For instance, is there any way believers can be separated from God again? Can children of God be un-reconciled again and thus not experience His fellowship? Eternally speaking, no.

> **Read 1 Corinthians 3:11-15.**
>
> [11] For no one can lay a foundation other than that which is laid, which is Jesus Christ. [12] Now if anyone builds on the foundation with gold, silver, precious stones, wood, hay, straw— [13] each one's work will become manifest, for the Day will disclose it, because it will be revealed by fire, and the fire will test what sort of work each one has done. [14] If the work that anyone has built on the foundation survives, he will receive a reward. [15] If anyone's work is burned up, he will suffer loss, though he himself will be saved, but only as through fire.

It is incredibly encouraging to know that once we are reconciled to God through His gift of forgiveness, we are forever so. Nothing can alter our changed position. We have received His forgiveness and are reconciled—and nothing can separate us from God's love.

LESSON 5:
WHAT IS RECONCILIATION? (PART 1)

Currently, in your daily living as a believer, are you experiencing His fellowship?
_____

The following verses explain what happens to believers who are not walking with God.

Read Romans 8:5-8.

5 For those who live according to the flesh set their minds on the things of the flesh, but those who live according to the Spirit set their minds on the things of the Spirit. 6 For to set the mind on the flesh is death, but to set the mind on the Spirit is life and peace. 7 For the mind that is set on the flesh is hostile to God, for it does not submit to God's law; indeed, it cannot. 8 Those who are in the flesh cannot please God.

_____
_____
_____
_____
_____

Read Psalm 78. (Read through the entire Psalm and write down the elements of sin that caused His children not to be reconciled to HIM.)

Tell the Coming Generation
A Maskil[a] of Asaph.
78 Give ear, O my people, to my teaching;
  incline your ears to the words of my mouth!
2 I will open my mouth in a parable;
  I will utter dark sayings from of old,
3 things that we have heard and known,
  that our fathers have told us.
4 We will not hide them from their children,
  but tell to the coming generation

LESSON 5:
WHAT IS RECONCILIATION? (PART 1)

   the glorious deeds of the Lord, and his might,
     and the wonders that he has done.
⁵ He established a testimony in Jacob
     and appointed a law in Israel,
which he commanded our fathers
     to teach to their children,
⁶ that the next generation might know them,
     the children yet unborn,
and arise and tell them to their children,
⁷ so that they should set their hope in God
and not forget the works of God,
     but keep his commandments;
⁸ and that they should not be like their fathers,
     a stubborn and rebellious generation,
a generation whose heart was not steadfast,
     whose spirit was not faithful to God.
⁹ The Ephraimites, armed with[b] the bow,
     turned back on the day of battle.
¹⁰ They did not keep God's covenant,
     but refused to walk according to his law.
¹¹ They forgot his works
     and the wonders that he had shown them.
¹² In the sight of their fathers he performed wonders
     in the land of Egypt, in the fields of Zoan.
¹³ He divided the sea and let them pass through it,
     and made the waters stand like a heap.
¹⁴ In the daytime he led them with a cloud,
     and all the night with a fiery light.
¹⁵ He split rocks in the wilderness
     and gave them drink abundantly as from the deep.
¹⁶ He made streams come out of the rock
     and caused waters to flow down like rivers.
¹⁷ Yet they sinned still more against him,
     rebelling against the Most High in the desert.
¹⁸ They tested God in their heart
     by demanding the food they craved.
¹⁹ They spoke against God, saying,
     "Can God spread a table in the wilderness?

LESSON 5:
WHAT IS RECONCILIATION? (PART 1)

20 He struck the rock so that water gushed out
 and streams overflowed.
Can he also give bread
 or provide meat for his people?"
21 Therefore, when the Lord heard, he was full of wrath;
 a fire was kindled against Jacob;
 his anger rose against Israel,
22 because they did not believe in God
 and did not trust his saving power.
23 Yet he commanded the skies above
 and opened the doors of heaven,
24 and he rained down on them manna to eat
 and gave them the grain of heaven.
25 Man ate of the bread of the angels;
 he sent them food in abundance.
26 He caused the east wind to blow in the heavens,
 and by his power he led out the south wind;
27 he rained meat on them like dust,
 winged birds like the sand of the seas;
28 he let them fall in the midst of their camp,
 all around their dwellings.
29 And they ate and were well filled,
 for he gave them what they craved.
30 But before they had satisfied their craving,
 while the food was still in their mouths,
31 the anger of God rose against them,
 and he killed the strongest of them
 and laid low the young men of Israel.
32 In spite of all this, they still sinned;
 despite his wonders, they did not believe.
33 So he made their days vanish like[c] a breath,[d]
 and their years in terror.
34 When he killed them, they sought him;
 they repented and sought God earnestly.
35 They remembered that God was their rock,
 the Most High God their redeemer.
36 But they flattered him with their mouths;
 they lied to him with their tongues.
37 Their heart was not steadfast toward him;

LESSON 5:
WHAT IS RECONCILIATION? (PART 1)

   they were not faithful to his covenant.
³⁸ Yet he, being compassionate,
   atoned for their iniquity
   and did not destroy them;
he restrained his anger often
   and did not stir up all his wrath.
³⁹ He remembered that they were but flesh,
   a wind that passes and comes not again.
⁴⁰ How often they rebelled against him in the wilderness
   and grieved him in the desert!
⁴¹ They tested God again and again
   and provoked the Holy One of Israel.
⁴² They did not remember his power[e]
   or the day when he redeemed them from the foe,
⁴³ when he performed his signs in Egypt
   and his marvels in the fields of Zoan.
⁴⁴ He turned their rivers to blood,
   so that they could not drink of their streams.
⁴⁵ He sent among them swarms of flies, which devoured them,
   and frogs, which destroyed them.
⁴⁶ He gave their crops to the destroying locust
   and the fruit of their labor to the locust.
⁴⁷ He destroyed their vines with hail
   and their sycamores with frost.
⁴⁸ He gave over their cattle to the hail
   and their flocks to thunderbolts.
⁴⁹ He let loose on them his burning anger,
   wrath, indignation, and distress,
   a company of destroying angels.
⁵⁰ He made a path for his anger;
   he did not spare them from death,
   but gave their lives over to the plague.
⁵¹ He struck down every firstborn in Egypt,
   the firstfruits of their strength in the tents of Ham.
⁵² Then he led out his people like sheep
   and guided them in the wilderness like a flock.
⁵³ He led them in safety, so that they were not afraid,
   but the sea overwhelmed their enemies.
⁵⁴ And he brought them to his holy land,

LESSON 5:
WHAT IS RECONCILIATION? (PART 1)

> to the mountain which his right hand had won.
> ⁵⁵ He drove out nations before them;
>   he apportioned them for a possession
>   and settled the tribes of Israel in their tents.
> ⁵⁶ Yet they tested and rebelled against the Most High God
>   and did not keep his testimonies,
> ⁵⁷ but turned away and acted treacherously like their fathers;
>   they twisted like a deceitful bow.
> ⁵⁸ For they provoked him to anger with their high places;
>   they moved him to jealousy with their idols.
> ⁵⁹ When God heard, he was full of wrath,
>   and he utterly rejected Israel.
> ⁶⁰ He forsook his dwelling at Shiloh,
>   the tent where he dwelt among mankind,
> ⁶¹ and delivered his power to captivity,
>   his glory to the hand of the foe.
> ⁶² He gave his people over to the sword
>   and vented his wrath on his heritage.
> ⁶³ Fire devoured their young men,
>   and their young women had no marriage song.
> ⁶⁴ Their priests fell by the sword,
>   and their widows made no lamentation.
> ⁶⁵ Then the Lord awoke as from sleep,
>   like a strong man shouting because of wine.
> ⁶⁶ And he put his adversaries to rout;
>   he put them to everlasting shame.
> ⁶⁷ He rejected the tent of Joseph;
>   he did not choose the tribe of Ephraim,
> ⁶⁸ but he chose the tribe of Judah,
>   Mount Zion, which he loves.
> ⁶⁹ He built his sanctuary like the high heavens,
>   like the earth, which he has founded forever.
> ⁷⁰ He chose David his servant
>   and took him from the sheepfolds;
> ⁷¹ from following the nursing ewes he brought him
>   to shepherd Jacob his people,
>   Israel his inheritance.
> ⁷² With upright heart he shepherded them
>   and guided them with his skillful hand.

LESSON 5:
WHAT IS RECONCILIATION? (PART 1)

_____
_____
_____
_____
_____

Remember the questions in the previous section:

- Is there any way believers can be separated from God again?

- Can children of God be un-reconciled again and thus not experience His fellowship?

Eternally speaking, we now know, the answer is no. However, we must understand that we can experience separation from God's fellowship in the present.

> **Read Isaiah 59:1-4.**
>
> Evil and Oppression
> **59** Behold, the Lord's hand is not shortened, that it cannot save,
>   or his ear dull, that it cannot hear;
> ² but your iniquities have made a separation
>   between you and your God,
> and your sins have hidden his face from you
>   so that he does not hear.
> ³ For your hands are defiled with blood
>   and your fingers with iniquity;
> your lips have spoken lies;
>   your tongue mutters wickedness.
> ⁴ No one enters suit justly;
>   no one goes to law honestly;
> they rely on empty pleas, they speak lies,
>   they conceive mischief and give birth to iniquity.

We as believers can be separated from God due to our iniquity, or sin, even though our eternal salvation is secure. Our unwillingness to walk in the Spirit and surrender our will to His will separates us from God's life, His fellowship. When this happens, we are in a position of being un-reconciled (loss of fellowship) within the

LESSON 5:
WHAT IS RECONCILIATION? (PART 1)

moment. In addition, when those circumstances arise putting the flesh before the Spirit, we also experience the three consequences of not being reconciled to God: quenching the Spirit (killing the life of the Holy Spirit in our lives), being at enmity against God (where we work in opposition to His will and believe He works against us), and being unable to please God. If this is not serious enough, our choice to walk directed by the self also prevents us from having our prayers heard by the Father, and we no longer live within the protection of His promises and benefits given to His reconciled children. We must be able to fully grasp these facts. A life lived in intimacy with God, fully receiving all of the benefits of being reconciled to the Creator does not come automatically. Instead, believers have a choice in how they live. They can either operate in the self, the carnal—as practical atheists living a life independent from God and experiencing the consequences of that life, or they can live within an intimate community and relationship with the Father. This may explain why so many believers live oppressed, difficult, harsh, and unpleasant lives…because they are unwilling to fully receive and live in forgiveness.

Write down what you have learned about the truths of reconciliation and the implications for us to be reconciled with God and for us to reconcile with others.

_____
_____
_____
_____
_____

Since it is possible to not be reconciled with God, what is the remedy? Read these verses and write down the remedies:

> **Read 1 John 1:9.**
>
> ⁹ If we confess our sins, he is faithful and just to forgive us our sins and to cleanse us from all unrighteousness.

_____
_____
_____
_____

LESSON 5:
WHAT IS RECONCILIATION? (PART 1)

Read Psalm 51.

Create in Me a Clean Heart, O God

To the choirmaster. A Psalm of David, when Nathan the prophet went to him, after he had gone in to Bathsheba.

51 Have mercy on me,[a] O God,
 according to your steadfast love;
according to your abundant mercy
 blot out my transgressions.
2 Wash me thoroughly from my iniquity,
 and cleanse me from my sin!
3 For I know my transgressions,
 and my sin is ever before me.
4 Against you, you only, have I sinned
 and done what is evil in your sight,
so that you may be justified in your words
 and blameless in your judgment.
5 Behold, I was brought forth in iniquity,
 and in sin did my mother conceive me.
6 Behold, you delight in truth in the inward being,
 and you teach me wisdom in the secret heart.
7 Purge me with hyssop, and I shall be clean;
 wash me, and I shall be whiter than snow.
8 Let me hear joy and gladness;
 let the bones that you have broken rejoice.
9 Hide your face from my sins,
 and blot out all my iniquities.
10 Create in me a clean heart, O God,
 and renew a right[b] spirit within me.
11 Cast me not away from your presence,
 and take not your Holy Spirit from me.
12 Restore to me the joy of your salvation,
 and uphold me with a willing spirit.
13 Then I will teach transgressors your ways,
 and sinners will return to you.

LESSON 5:
WHAT IS RECONCILIATION? (PART 1)

> ¹⁴ Deliver me from bloodguiltiness, O God,
>   O God of my salvation,
>   and my tongue will sing aloud of your righteousness.
> ¹⁵ O Lord, open my lips,
>   and my mouth will declare your praise.
> ¹⁶ For you will not delight in sacrifice, or I would give it;
>   you will not be pleased with a burnt offering.
> ¹⁷ The sacrifices of God are a broken spirit;
>   a broken and contrite heart, O God, you will not despise.
> ¹⁸ Do good to Zion in your good pleasure;
>   build up the walls of Jerusalem;
> ¹⁹ then will you delight in right sacrifices,
>   in burnt offerings and whole burnt offerings;
>   then bulls will be offered on your altar.

_____
_____
_____
_____
_____

> **Read 2 Chronicles 7:14-15.**
>
> ¹⁴ if my people who are called by my name humble themselves, and pray and seek my face and turn from their wicked ways, then I will hear from heaven and will forgive their sin and heal their land. ¹⁵ Now my eyes will be open and my ears attentive to the prayer that is made in this place.

_____
_____
_____
_____
_____

LESSON 5:
WHAT IS RECONCILIATION? (PART 1)

> **Read Deuteronomy 10:12-14.**
>
> Circumcise Your Heart
> [12] "And now, Israel, what does the Lord your God require of you, but to fear the Lord your God, to walk in all his ways, to love him, to serve the Lord your God with all your heart and with all your soul, [13] and to keep the commandments and statutes of the Lord, which I am commanding you today for your good? [14] Behold, to the Lord your God belong heaven and the heaven of heavens, the earth with all that is in it.

_____
_____
_____
_____
_____

We learn here that we are to:

- Fear Him
- Walk in His ways
- Love Him with all heart and soul
- Serve Him
- Follow His instructions; surrender my will to His

What is the result?

_____
_____
_____
_____
_____

(Restored fellowship with Him)

LESSON 5:
WHAT IS RECONCILIATION? (PART 1)

Is this always available? _____ *(Yes)*

How many times can this happen? _____ *(Endlessly)*

Read Matthew 18:21-22.

The Parable of the Unforgiving Servant
[21] Then Peter came up and said to him, "Lord, how often will my brother sin against me, and I forgive him? As many as seven times?" [22] Jesus said to him, "I do not say to you seven times, but seventy-seven times.

Does He alter the truth for us to experience this restoration?
_____ *(No)*

Resolution requires that two parties process truth and come to a resolution satisfactory to both parties.

As just mentioned, those who have been reconciled, believers, followers of Christ, have a continual choice in how to live. If we choose to live in the Spirit, our relationship with God is close and nothing impedes communication between the two. However, if we do not choose to live in the Spirit, we are choosing by default to live in the flesh, in the self. This means our relationship with God is temporarily broken. Once again, sin and self separate the Creator from His creation, but it is only in terms of fellowship, not of position. The remedy, again, is simple. We need to be reconciled to His truth. We need reconciliation to God's heart. Remember, He has already completed the work of forgiveness, and we are forgiven. This is no problem for Him, but for instant reconciliation, repentance and confession play a key role. It is essential to tell God how we have been walking according to the flesh and then repent of our behavior, and He will forgive us.

Throughout these Scriptures we are told to "fear God," that this fear of the Almighty is required in our repentance. However, the fear described here needs an explanation. Most of the time when we fear something, such fears are defined as being scared, having dread toward something, or fear causing anxiety on our part. When Scripture tells us to fear God, it in no means intends for us to have dread toward God. God is loving and forgiving. Remember how we talked about His nature? That He cannot help but forgive? That God is holy? According to the definition of the Hebrew word, the fear of the Lord means to stand in awe of, to revere, to honor and respect God. This is done when we acknowledge our Creator as all powerful, all mighty, and all-knowing, and we are not. This acknowledgment

LESSON 5:
WHAT IS RECONCILIATION? (PART 1)

of God's position and character puts us in our rightful position of needing His wisdom, power, care, and forgiveness. In short, we recognize we cannot live apart from Him, from the Spirit. Fearing God also means we believe His Word is true and that all He speaks through His Word is true and available to you, to me, to us. Stop debating and doubting whether or not what you hear from the Word is true and instead process the confusion and questions further with God until clarity is experienced. Then, stand in awe and reverence of God most holy and recognize that by following His words you will receive blessings, but a refusal to hear and follow will have you experience negative consequences.

Next, we are told to walk in God's ways. In order to do this, we must choose to die to our self (our self-agenda, our self-centeredness, etc.) and allow God's Spirit to work through us, living fully in us. When we choose to walk with Him instead of our own selfish ways, when we surrender our will to His will, when we desire to truly hear what He wants to say to us, then we can walk in God's ways. Then we are able to follow Him as He leads and guides us, step by step, day by day, and can remain on His path, not our own. Denying our flesh, following God's instructions for our life, surrendering our will to Christ's is how we live life to the fullest, receiving the abundant life Jesus came to give! Is it difficult? That denying of our flesh certainly does not come naturally, but the more we do it, the easier it becomes to follow Christ in all fullness. Here is an example:

At one of our retreats, there was a young couple who had been married a few years. The husband was a financial planner, and she was an aspiring country music songwriter. She would travel back and forth to Nashville attempting to break into the business, and he worked hard to build his local practice. They wanted to have children but were waiting. They felt as though their financial position would not allow them to manage a family and were unsure of where to put down roots while having so many questions about work, family, etc. They had a strained marriage, but not because they were angry at each other. Instead, the strain was experienced because they each had a concept of what life should be like and were not taking the time to work it through together to a consensus. No couple can learn to walk with God in the Spirit with unresolved conflict or unfulfilled expectations festering in their souls. At all of our retreats we spend significant time discussing how to abide in Christ, how to walk in the Spirit, how to surrender our will to His, and how to seek His best for us. There, they agreed they had been living their lives engaged in their own self-centeredness. Upon this realization, they decided to learn a new way, surrendering their will to the Father's. What first happened was they were released of the pressure of trying to figure everything out. They decided to live life in unity, on the same side of the table, and to have God reveal and show His will to them. They began enjoying abiding, sharing the truths that God was revealing to them, and seeking the wisdom of God in all

LESSON 5:
WHAT IS RECONCILIATION? (PART 1)

their decisions. For two years God revealed His will to them step by step. The wife received an international songwriting contract from a firm located in Los Angeles, and his work continued to thrive locally. Because of the opportunities from her new management company, she is fully endorsed and able to establish roots in their hometown. They are cleared by God to begin a family. They have been led to sell the condo, (which sold the first day listed), and bought a new home in the suburbs. Their marriage is continuing to flourish as they, together, abide in the vine and walk in the Spirit. Their life has changed to one full of joy and wonder, and they are beginning to "give it away" to their friends who have seen the change in their life and have a desire to learn what it means to walk in the Spirit—all because they made a decision to surrender their will to God, deny themselves, and take up the cross to follow Him.

Was it difficult for this couple to deny their self-will, both individually and collectively? Any time anyone denies their flesh, a struggle will ensue. However, this couple made a choice to leave the decision-making to God in their marriage and in their lives, and it was worth every struggle. So, yes denying the self is hard, but in comparison with the joy of following Christ in an intimate and abiding relationship, there is no sorrow. However, denial of the flesh is only one aspect of following Christ.

Another important aspect of walking with God, is to love God with all of our heart and soul. And, we know that even that is impossible apart from Christ fully living within us; that conscious decision to walk in the Spirit. Walking every moment there naturally develops that deep affection toward being with Christ, caring for and with Him, and simply enjoying His presence and His affection toward you, His dearly loved child. Such affection and love are communicated through communion, prayer, scripture reading, etc. Basically, the more time you choose to walk in the Spirit, the more you fall in love with Jesus. The more you fall in love with Jesus, the more time you spend with Him, talking with Him. The more time you spend with Him, the more you choose to walk in the Spirit and be led and guided by it. Eventually you get to the point where you ask yourself, "Why, in light of how much He loves me and I love Him, would I do anything else?"

What else are we to do as Christ followers? We are called to serve our King. When you walk in the Spirit, you see your role as serving God and His desires instead of your own will. When we have a heart already surrendered to His will, our servant's heart will desire nothing more than to join Him where He is at work, knowing fully His will and His direction for your life, my life, is better than anything we could ever imagine. And finally, God calls us to follow His instructions. While living directed by God's Spirit living within you, your heart to follow God's commands as it relates to you personally will be one of obedience. To the best of your ability, you take each step laid before you in faith, knowing the promises associated with each step of obedience will be fulfilled by the promise keeper.

> "...the more time you choose to walk in the Spirit, the more you fall in love with Jesus."

LESSON 5:
WHAT IS RECONCILIATION? (PART 1)

> "Holiness is a result of our living life freed from sin through His forgiveness, and then us surrendering our lives to Him with a heart to serve Him completely."

This is a big area of consternation for most believers. We are taught that in order to receive God's favor we must be obedient and follow the precepts and instructions in Scripture. We think if we were able to perform a good portion of God's precepts (we know we cannot keep them all), we then hope we are good enough to obtain blessing and favor. We still see God as a lawgiver, distant from us, requiring us to be holy and righteous. We have it all backwards. Righteousness is Christ, and we can only become righteous by putting on Christ. Furthermore, holiness is a fruit, not something we achieve. Rather, it is a result of our relationship with Christ. Romans 6 gives us an interesting progression regarding experiencing holiness. Verse 7 says, "For he who has died has been freed from sin,"—done deal, past tense. Verse 18 builds upon that and says, "And having been set free from sin, you became slaves of righteousness" (we surrendered our will to His and have an intimate relationship with Him). Verse 22 completes the progression, "But now having been set free from sin, and having become slaves of God, you have your fruit to holiness, and the end, everlasting life." Holiness is a result of our living life freed from sin through His forgiveness, and then us surrendering our lives to Him with a heart to serve Him completely. As we do, we then have a love and a heart relationship to follow Him, knowing that His will is best and none better. Our love grows, our intimacy grows, and our obedience is fulfilled through His power in us out of our heart love for Him. It is much like that of a toddler to his parents. A toddler naturally has an affection for his parents, and through the loving instruction and care of the parents, learns to willingly obey the parents' instructions. He or she quickly learns that things go better when he or she obeys the parents. In the same way, obeying the Father is a true joy and is done out of our heart relationship, not as a duty.

So, how is your walk with the Father? Are you walking in that joyful experience that is an abiding relationship in the vine? Are you presently separated from a close relationship with God? If so, there is wonderful news for you…you can have a restored and reconciled relationship beginning right now! Repent and turn from your flesh, from the self, and turn toward God in faith and trust. Walk in the Spirit one step at a time, one day at a time, and get up every time you fall. This is the beginning of life's greatest adventure and fulfillment.

So, let's say you have wandered away from walking in the Spirit, that your sin has separated you from the fellowship of God once experienced. Now what? The answer is the same: repent and believe. Once we admit our sin to God, that we have missed the mark God set for us, He will forgive us because He is faithful to His word and promises. Our fellowship with our Creator is completely restored. Is this restoration always available? Yes. How many times can we possibly expect to be forgiven of our sin, our shortcomings? God's forgiveness is endless. He will forgive us as many times as we sincerely ask for it.

LESSON 5:
WHAT IS RECONCILIATION? (PART 1)

Matthew 18:21-22 are interesting passages. Jewish tradition taught people to forgive their offenders three times and no more. So, when Peter spoke the number seven, more than double the number expected of a "good Jewish man," he was asking if human forgiveness should be exercised to such a great extent. The number seven also had spiritual connotations, meaning the fullness of perfection. So, in a way, Peter was also asking what the perfect solution was to how often man should be forgiven by another. Jesus' response spoke of God's offering of forgiveness to humanity, and our reply as mere humans in turn. The seventy times seven denotes an endless supply of God's forgiveness toward us, His creation. And since He first forgave us, we are to offer endless forgiveness to those who offend us. In a simple mathematical equation, Jesus confounded the wisdom of Jewish tradition by multiplying the expectation for our reaction to wrongs done to us far beyond what anyone had previously thought. And the reason for such a shockingly large number? Because God forgives us all the more. Remember, because God is faithful and just, He cleanses us instantaneously (1 John 1:9) each and every time He forgives us and therefore, there is nothing for us to fix. We need to merely return and be restored. Christ tells us there are no limits to His forgiveness. It is day by day, moment by moment, and there is endless opportunity to be reconciled. So how does this apply to everyday life, to you, to me?

If you had a brother or sister who agreed to meet you for lunch and then failed to show up, you would certainly be upset but probably forgive them. If it happened a second time, you would be more upset but could probably forgive them again. However, if it happened a third time we would basically say, "That's enough, I am done with this" and struggle to forgive them further, right? In our natural life, we have limitations as to how much we can take. Perhaps this will help us understand the depth of Christ nature: endless forgiveness with no limitations. And if He has endless forgiveness toward us, through Him, we can have endless forgiveness toward others.

Experiencing Restoration

How does this relate to reconciliation? We recall that Christ never alters the truth in order for us to experience restoration and reconciliation. We can stay un-reconciled and live outside of an intimate relationship with Him, outside of the benefits of living in this relationship.

LESSON 5:
WHAT IS RECONCILIATION? (PART 1)

> **Read Hebrews 3:15-19.**
>
> [15] As it is said,
>
> "Today, if you hear his voice,
> do not harden your hearts as in the rebellion."
>
> [16] For who were those who heard and yet rebelled? Was it not all those who left Egypt led by Moses? [17] And with whom was he provoked for forty years? Was it not with those who sinned, whose bodies fell in the wilderness? [18] And to whom did he swear that they would not enter his rest, but to those who were disobedient? [19] So we see that they were unable to enter because of unbelief.

The Israelites who had been "saved" through the parting of the Red Sea were given a promise by God. His will was for them to enter the Promised Land, and He told the Israelites He would defeat their enemies and deliver them into all of the benefits of living in the Promised Land. However, they refused to go because of fear. They refused to believe God would fulfill His promises, and it was this unbelief that led to God's anger toward them. God was angry with that generation and allowed them to wander in the wilderness for 40 years and refused to let the unfaithful enter into the land He had promised. Those people died outside of the good and perfect will of God. God in no way altered the truth so that generation could enter into the Promised Land. Those Israelites were not willing to fully process the truth of God's promises despite their fear, and they remained un-reconciled to God and suffered the consequences of such. However, God did not abandon His chosen people. He provided His presence in a cloud by day and a pillar of fire by night, both for their protection. He gave them manna each morning, quail to eat, plenty of water to drink, and neither their clothing nor their shoes ever wore out—for 40 years! God still provided for them because He never stopped loving them. Their status as God's chosen people was secure, just like our eternal salvation is secure upon our initial repenting and believing, but they lived their lives apart from the intimate relationship God offered to them and wanted to have with them. Instead, they lived out the remainder of their years wandering around aimlessly in the wilderness and never received the promises God spoke to them. God offered

LESSON 5:
WHAT IS RECONCILIATION? (PART 1)

reconciliation, but they did not receive the offer, and therefore, reconciliation never happened. Reconciliation necessitates two parties to both process truth and a resolution satisfactory to both parties must be accepted. With it, reconciliation happens. Without it, reconciliation will not happen.

Have you received this reconciliation from God? Are there others in your life you need to offer reconciliation to today? Remember, we are called to offer forgiveness to others as Christ offers forgiveness to the world—at all times and without condition. Regarding those who have hurt you, pray for God to give you the strength to forgive them, then forgive them. Do not allow your self-will to rule. Walk in God's Spirit and forgive them in His power, releasing them to God and then opening yourself up to absolute freedom with the Father.

_____
_____
_____
_____
_____
_____
_____
_____
_____
_____
_____
_____
_____
_____
_____
_____
_____
_____
_____
_____
_____

LESSON 5:
WHAT IS RECONCILIATION? (PART 1)

LESSON 6:
WHAT IS RECONCILIATION? (PART 2)

What are the benefits of reconciliation? Read through the following verses and write out the wonderful benefits that we receive from being reconciled to Christ.

Redemption means that life is returned to us.

> **Read Ephesians 1:7-12.**
>
> ⁷ In him we have redemption through his blood, the forgiveness of our trespasses, according to the riches of his grace, ⁸ which he lavished upon us, in all wisdom and insight ⁹ making known[a] to us the mystery of his will, according to his purpose, which he set forth in Christ ¹⁰ as a plan for the fullness of time, to unite all things in him, things in heaven and things on earth.
>
> ¹¹ In him we have obtained an inheritance, having been predestined according to the purpose of him who works all things according to the counsel of his will, ¹² so that we who were the first to hope in Christ might be to the praise of his glory.

> "When we allow God to pursue us, His life in us brings wholeness, fullness, and goodness."

_____
_____
_____
_____
_____
_____
_____
_____
_____

LESSON 6:
WHAT IS RECONCILIATION? (PART 2)

> **Read 1 Corinthians 1:26-31.**
>
> [26] For consider your calling, brothers: not many of you were wise according to worldly standards,[a] not many were powerful, not many were of noble birth. [27] But God chose what is foolish in the world to shame the wise; God chose what is weak in the world to shame the strong; [28] God chose what is low and despised in the world, even things that are not, to bring to nothing things that are, [29] so that no human being[b] might boast in the presence of God. [30] And because of him[c] you are in Christ Jesus, who became to us wisdom from God, righteousness and sanctification and redemption, [31] so that, as it is written, "Let the one who boasts, boast in the Lord."

_____
_____
_____
_____
_____

When we allow God to pursue us, His life in us brings wholeness, fullness, and goodness.

Through His righteousness (and not our own), we are given the strength to pursue those things He has for us, especially, in this case, the power to move toward forgiveness and reconciliation.

> **Read 1 John 1:9.**
>
> [9] If we confess our sins, he is faithful and just to forgive us our sins and to cleanse us from all unrighteousness.

_____
_____
_____
_____
_____

LESSON 6:
WHAT IS RECONCILIATION? (PART 2)

> **Read Romans 3:24-25.**
>
> ²⁴ and are justified by his grace as a gift, through the redemption that is in Christ Jesus,²⁵ whom God put forward as a propitiation by his blood, to be received by faith. This was to show God's righteousness, because in his divine forbearance he had passed over former sins.

_____
_____
_____
_____
_____

We cannot earn it or achieve it—just receive it and live in it.

> **Guidance: Read Psalm 32:8-9.**
>
> ⁸ I will instruct you and teach you in the way you should go;
>   I will counsel you with my eye upon you.
> ⁹ Be not like a horse or a mule, without understanding,
>   which must be curbed with bit and bridle,
>   or it will not stay near you.

_____
_____
_____
_____
_____

We have the privilege of having our lives directed by the sovereign God who knows all, has all power and might, and desires to give us the best!

LESSON 6:
WHAT IS RECONCILIATION? (PART 2)

> **Joy: Read Psalm 32:10-11.**
>
> ¹⁰ Many are the sorrows of the wicked,
>   but steadfast love surrounds the one who trusts in the Lord.
> ¹¹ Be glad in the Lord, and rejoice, O righteous,
>   and shout for joy, all you upright in heart!

_____
_____
_____
_____
_____

We are given through God not worldly joy that is fleeting, but eternal, spiritual joy that fills our life with Him and the wonder and awe of daily walking with Him.

> **He forgets our failure: Read Psalm 103:12.**
>
> ¹² as far as the east is from the west,
>   so far does he remove our transgressions from us.

_____
_____
_____
_____
_____

> **Read Hebrews 10:17.**
>
> ⁷ then he adds,
> "I will remember their sins and their lawless deeds no more."

LESSON 6:
WHAT IS RECONCILIATION? (PART 2)

Every time is a "do over." We are given the opportunity to try life again. God forgets our failures and asks us to just walk with Him anew and receive the beautiful life planned.

> **Power: Read Ephesians 1:15-23.**
>
> Thanksgiving and Prayer
> [15] For this reason, because I have heard of your faith in the Lord Jesus and your love[a] toward all the saints, [16] I do not cease to give thanks for you, remembering you in my prayers, [17] that the God of our Lord Jesus Christ, the Father of glory, may give you the Spirit of wisdom and of revelation in the knowledge of him, [18] having the eyes of your hearts enlightened, that you may know what is the hope to which he has called you, what are the riches of his glorious inheritance in the saints, [19] and what is the immeasurable greatness of his power toward us who believe, according to the working of his great might [20] that he worked in Christ when he raised him from the dead and seated him at his right hand in the heavenly places, [21] far above all rule and authority and power and dominion, and above every name that is named, not only in this age but also in the one to come. [22] And he put all things under his feet and gave him as head over all things to the church, [23] which is his body, the fullness of him who fills all in all.

LESSON 6:
WHAT IS RECONCILIATION? (PART 2)

> **Read Ephesians 3:14-21.**
>
> Prayer for Spiritual Strength
> 14 For this reason I bow my knees before the Father, 15 from whom every family[a] in heaven and on earth is named, 16 that according to the riches of his glory he may grant you to be strengthened with power through his Spirit in your inner being, 17 so that Christ may dwell in your hearts through faith—that you, being rooted and grounded in love, 18 may have strength to comprehend with all the saints what is the breadth and length and height and depth, 19 and to know the love of Christ that surpasses knowledge, that you may be filled with all the fullness of God.
>
> 20 Now to him who is able to do far more abundantly than all that we ask or think, according to the power at work within us, 21 to him be glory in the church and in Christ Jesus throughout all generations, forever and ever. Amen.

_____
_____
_____
_____
_____

God desires to do supernatural things in our lives and in our circumstances and to demonstrate the wonder and awe of His power through us.

> **Peace: Read John 14:25-27.**
>
> 25 "These things I have spoken to you while I am still with you. 26 But the Helper, the Holy Spirit, whom the Father will send in my name, he will teach you all things and bring to your remembrance all that I have said to you. 27 Peace I leave with you; my peace I give to you. Not as the world gives do I give to you. Let not your hearts be troubled, neither let them be afraid.

LESSON 6:
WHAT IS RECONCILIATION? (PART 2)

Read Acts: 18-23. (When time allows, work through the stories of how Paul lived in complete peace despite all the interesting and difficult circumstances he faced. He completely trusted in and remained reconciled to God—all the time, every time.)

_____
_____
_____
_____
_____
_____
_____
_____
_____

As with joy, our life with God is not a fleeting peace of the world. It is an eternal peace from Him, as we rest in Him, surrender to Him, and know that He will give us His peace to enjoy every day, despite whatever circumstances we face.

> **Mercy, Kindness, and Tenderness: Read Psalm 103:4; 103:8-9.**
>
> ⁴ who redeems your life from the pit,
>   who crowns you with steadfast love and mercy,
>
> ⁸ The Lord is merciful and gracious,
>   slow to anger and abounding in steadfast love.
> ⁹ He will not always chide,
>   nor will he keep his anger forever.

_____
_____
_____
_____

LESSON 6:
WHAT IS RECONCILIATION? (PART 2)

> **Read Psalm 130:7-8.**
>
> ⁷ O Israel, hope in the Lord!
>   For with the Lord there is steadfast love,
>   and with him is plentiful redemption.
> ⁸ And he will redeem Israel
>   from all his iniquities.

_____
_____
_____
_____
_____

> **Read Ephesians 4:31-32.**
>
> ³¹ Let all bitterness and wrath and anger and clamor and slander be put away from you, along with all malice. ³² Be kind to one another, tenderhearted, forgiving one another, as God in Christ forgave you.

_____
_____
_____
_____
_____

Our hearts will not go to anger, hardness, bitterness, or edginess, but rather will be living with mercy, kindness, and tenderness, the soft qualities of His nature in us that give us freedom, joy, and peace, especially in a very dark and difficult world, filled with selfish people.

LESSON 6:
WHAT IS RECONCILIATION? (PART 2)

> **Healing: Read Psalm 103:3.**
>
> ³ who forgives all your iniquity,
>   who heals all your diseases…

_____
_____
_____
_____
_____

We will experience His supernatural healing of our emotions, our soul, and our physical life.

> **Restored from destructive patterns: Read Psalm 103:4.**
>
> ⁴ who redeems your life from the pit,
> who crowns you with steadfast love and mercy…

_____
_____
_____
_____
_____

He will change our typical destructive patterns that respond in fear, anxiety, anger, wrath, hardness, etc. to trust and peace. This is not some new learned behavior, but a true transformation where the pattern is released, and a new way of life restored in its place.

LESSON 6:
WHAT IS RECONCILIATION? (PART 2)

> **To feel the satisfaction that comes with good things (renewal), read Psalm 103:5.**
>
> ⁵ who satisfies you with good
>   so that your youth is renewed like the eagle's.

_____
_____
_____
_____
_____

He desires to give us and have us experience good things in our lives. His best for us contributes to a life of freedom, joy, and peace.

Write down what you have learned about the truths of reconciliation, the benefits of reconciliation, and the implications for us to be reconciled with God and for us to reconcile with others.

_____
_____
_____
_____
_____
_____
_____
_____
_____
_____

LESSON 6:
WHAT IS RECONCILIATION? (PART 2)

These are just but a few of over 7,000 promises and benefits spoken to us, and for us in Scripture.

God desires us to experience all of His goodness and rewards. After all, Jesus came into the world not to condemn it or to provide another list of tasks to accomplish, but He came to give us life, and give it in abundance. God's nature is for us to not only live life but to enjoy it to the fullest. When we live our lives in perpetual forgiveness toward others, we can live this abundant life and reap all of its benefits. In fact, living with such benefits is the very indication that we have been restored to a whole and immensely beautiful relationship with God. We become the living and walking testimonies of God's redemptive work offered to all of humanity. The same thing can be said of the benefits of living in restored relationships with our friends, families, and co-workers. When we are forgiven and live in the fullness of being forgiven, we can offer forgiveness freely to others. And yet, when we slip and live ruled by our flesh, our relationships with those around us are conflicted, jarred, and distant. We must remember to live with a Kingdom mentality. When we live Kingdom-minded, living as residents of a heavenly realm, we walk in the Spirit and experience all of the life available from our King. When we live according to our self, we operate outside of the benefits, life, and protection of the Kingdom.

Take a moment to meditate on the Scriptures listed above. Allow God's truth to sink deeply into your heart as you learn the benefits of reconciliation. Listen to the Spirit, through God's Word, whisper to you and give you life. Believe it, embrace it, and walk in its light.

The Lord desires us to fully understand all these truths of forgiveness and reconciliation by living a life of always forgiving others. It is actually an indication to us that we are living a restored life into the beautiful relationship with Him and thus experiencing all the benefits of that restored relationship. We must operate on the same basis. If we have forgiveness toward others, it is because we are living in God's forgiveness for us. If we do not have forgiveness for others, it means we are not living in God's forgiveness for us, which means we are not living in the "Kingdom," experiencing all the life and benefits of the Kingdom. Rather, we are operating in self, on our own, outside the Kingdom.

We can forgive because we are receiving and living in His nature, which is forgiveness; and we stand in peace and freedom, ready and willing to reconcile—and until we are able to approach reconciliation with forgiveness—living in peace and freedom; we will not be able to truly reconcile.

Work through the following verses that help define the necessity of forgiveness and how we are to process reconciliation with others. What is the impact if we do not forgive?

LESSON 6:
WHAT IS RECONCILIATION? (PART 2)

> **Read Galatians 5:19-21.**
>
> [19] Now the works of the flesh are evident: sexual immorality, impurity, sensuality, [20] idolatry, sorcery, enmity, strife, jealousy, fits of anger, rivalries, dissensions, divisions, [21] envy,[a] drunkenness, orgies, and things like these. I warn you, as I warned you before, that those who do[b] such things will not inherit the kingdom of God.

_____
_____
_____
_____
_____

    Recall that in order for true reconciliation to occur between us and other people, we must first be reconciled to God. We must live out the simplicity of reconciliation—knowing that we are forgiven (already done and complete, which is no problem for Him), and then process the truth that He offers to process with us until we reach agreement. Once reconciliation between us and God happens, then reconciliation between us and our offenders can take place on the same basis. We first forgive them (between us and God—on the same basis that He forgave us, through His nature), and then offer to process the truth until we reach agreement and thus reconciliation. Remember, through living in the Spirit, we have the ability to forgive others where in the flesh we do not. When we receive and are abiding in His forgiving nature, we stand firm in the peace and freedom only God Himself can give. Walking in the liberty available through Christ only comes as a result of us being ready and willing to reconcile to God in the first place. Remember, we have to repent and believe: We have to believe God exists, that He is good, that He wants to forgive us, and then accept the gift so unreservedly offered. However, if we continually refuse to seek the true reconciliation, which only comes through forgiveness, living in God's peace and freedom will be unattainable. Reconciliation is not possible without forgiveness, and we then reap the consequences of un-forgiveness.

LESSON 6:
WHAT IS RECONCILIATION? (PART 2)

Read Hebrews 12:14-17.

[14] Strive for peace with everyone, and for the holiness without which no one will see the Lord. [15] See to it that no one fails to obtain the grace of God; that no "root of bitterness" springs up and causes trouble, and by it many become defiled; [16] that no one is sexually immoral or unholy like Esau, who sold his birthright for a single meal. [17] For you know that afterward, when he desired to inherit the blessing, he was rejected, for he found no chance to repent, though he sought it with tears.

Read Galatians 5:1-6.

Christ Has Set Us Free
5 For freedom Christ has set us free; stand firm therefore, and do not submit again to a yoke of slavery.

[2] Look: I, Paul, say to you that if you accept circumcision, Christ will be of no advantage to you. [3] I testify again to every man who accepts circumcision that he is obligated to keep the whole law. [4] You are severed from Christ, you who would be justified[a] by the law; you have fallen away from grace. [5] For through the Spirit, by faith, we ourselves eagerly wait for the hope of righteousness. [6] For in Christ Jesus neither circumcision nor uncircumcision counts for anything, but only faith working through love.

Read Romans 1:24-32.

[24] Therefore God gave them up in the lusts of their hearts to impurity, to the dishonoring of their bodies among themselves, [25] because they exchanged the truth about God for a lie and worshiped and served the creature rather than the Creator, who is blessed forever! Amen.

[26] For this reason God gave them up to dishonorable passions. For their women exchanged natural relations for those that are contrary to nature; [27] and the men likewise gave up natural relations with women and were consumed with passion for one another, men committing shameless acts with men and receiving in themselves the due penalty for their error.

LESSON 6:
WHAT IS RECONCILIATION? (PART 2)

> [28] And since they did not see fit to acknowledge God, God gave them up to a debased mind to do what ought not to be done. [29] They were filled with all manner of unrighteousness, evil, covetousness, malice. They are full of envy, murder, strife, deceit, maliciousness. They are gossips, [30] slanderers, haters of God, insolent, haughty, boastful, inventors of evil, disobedient to parents, [31] foolish, faithless, heartless, ruthless. [32] Though they know God's righteous decree that those who practice such things deserve to die, they not only do them but give approval to those who practice them.

When we maintain un-forgiveness, our anger is maintained, not resolved, and bitterness is the evil result. This bitterness is a clear indication someone has chosen to live in the flesh, they have not surrendered their will to the Father, and are not willing to walk with God on the path He has chosen for them. There are serious consequences to such behavior. Such a person, including us from time to time if we are honest, is again placed under the bondage of the law and is required to keep the entirety of it. Since no one can keep the entire law in and of themselves, they fall from God's grace and become estranged from the personal and intimate relationship with Christ. Only within that wonderful relationship can we have all of our needs provided for and the power received to live the life of forgiveness. When any believer chooses to walk by the flesh, ruled by the flesh, they develop characteristics indicative of the world: anger, wrath, evil speaking, hardness, deceitful, backbiting, arguers, etc., and their life is lived in a constant sense of disappointment, oppression, and resignation. Think about it. How many of us have been in a group of our friends, or even in church, and have heard others gossiping about someone? How many times have you lost your temper getting your children ready to go to church? How about friendships which are lost over petty issues? How many of us have heard of a church splitting over the color of carpet to go in the sanctuary or some other irrelevant matter? Unfortunately, these and many more are a result of not living and walking in the Spirit. Can you now see why forgiveness is such a crucial issue to resolve in your own life? No one intentionally wants to sabotage their own happiness, joy, or peace, but those who refuse to forgive and continue to walk according to the flesh end up doing just that. Forgiveness is not something we simply do in order to meet any type of spiritual requirement, and it is certainly nothing we can accomplish on our own. Rather, forgiveness is an indicator of if and how we are walking guided by the Spirit and walking with our Father in the same way backbiting, being argumentative, harshness, and wrath are indicators of the opposite. When God's

LESSON 6:
WHAT IS RECONCILIATION? (PART 2)

children are close to their Father and are living in the gift of forgiveness they have so eagerly received, that very nature of God living in us allows us to quickly and readily forgive others.

> **How will we actually know we are living in forgiveness? Read Colossians 3:12-17.**
>
> [12] Put on then, as God's chosen ones, holy and beloved, compassionate hearts, kindness, humility, meekness, and patience, [13] bearing with one another and, if one has a complaint against another, forgiving each other; as the Lord has forgiven you, so you also must forgive. [14] And above all these put on love, which binds everything together in perfect harmony. [15] And let the peace of Christ rule in your hearts, to which indeed you were called in one body. And be thankful. [16] Let the word of Christ dwell in you richly, teaching and admonishing one another in all wisdom, singing psalms and hymns and spiritual songs, with thankfulness in your hearts to God. [17] And whatever you do, in word or deed, do everything in the name of the Lord Jesus, giving thanks to God the Father through him.

_____
_____
_____
_____
_____

We will know we are in forgiveness when the thought of someone, or the name of someone mentioning that person, or having contact with someone do not bring us to anger, resentment, or a bitterness that brings us to a desire for withdrawal or revenge:

- We can be in same room as that person and remain in peace and freedom.

- We can intercede for that person, asking God for the best for that person.

LESSON 6:
WHAT IS RECONCILIATION? (PART 2)

> **Read 2 Timothy 2:20-26.**
>
> [20] Now in a great house there are not only vessels of gold and silver but also of wood and clay, some for honorable use, some for dishonorable. [21] Therefore, if anyone cleanses himself from what is dishonorable,[a] he will be a vessel for honorable use, set apart as holy, useful to the master of the house, ready for every good work.
>
> [22] So flee youthful passions and pursue righteousness, faith, love, and peace, along with those who call on the Lord from a pure heart. [23] Have nothing to do with foolish, ignorant controversies; you know that they breed quarrels. [24] And the Lord's servant[b] must not be quarrelsome but kind to everyone, able to teach, patiently enduring evil, [25] correcting his opponents with gentleness. God may perhaps grant them repentance leading to a knowledge of the truth, [26] and they may come to their senses and escape from the snare of the devil, after being captured by him to do his will.

_____
_____
_____
_____
_____

    God's call to us is to live a life of continual forgiveness as well as to constantly offer reconciliation to others. But remember, forgiveness is separate from reconciliation. Our part is to first forgive others on the same basis God has forgiven us, not based upon what mere humanity deserves. God's loving and forgiving nature gives us the power to maintain His forgiving character through us to be offered in all circumstances and to all the people around us. But, when we live in such darkness because we are ruled by our flesh, forgiveness cannot be offered to others. If we fail to stay connected to the author of forgiveness, then offering it is impossible. So, how do we know if we are living according to God's forgiving nature?

    Simply explained, we will know by our actions and reactions. When we think about someone who has hurt us, or their name is brought up in conversation and we no longer associate them with bitterness, we are walking in the Spirit.

LESSON 6:
WHAT IS RECONCILIATION? (PART 2)

When we do not become angry or resentful of them for what they have done, we are walking in the Spirit. When we do not desire revenge or a need to withdraw from them, it is by the Spirit we are being led. When we know we are able to be in the same room with our offender and can remain in peace and freedom, God's Spirit is leading us. When we can intercede for the one who wounded us and genuinely pray for the best God has for them, we are walking in the Spirit. How do we know? Because all of those actions are a result of forgiving them the wrong they did to you.

> **Read Job 22:21-30.**
>
> [21] "Agree with God, and be at peace;
>   thereby good will come to you.
> [22] Receive instruction from his mouth,
>   and lay up his words in your heart.
> [23] If you return to the Almighty you will be built up;
>   if you remove injustice far from your tents,
> [24] if you lay gold in the dust,
>   and gold of Ophir among the stones of the torrent-bed,
> [25] then the Almighty will be your gold
>   and your precious silver.
> [26] For then you will delight yourself in the Almighty
>   and lift up your face to God.
> [27] You will make your prayer to him, and he will hear you,
>   and you will pay your vows.
> [28] You will decide on a matter, and it will be established for you,
>   and light will shine on your ways.
> [29] For when they are humbled you say, 'It is because of pride';[a]
>   but he saves the lowly.
> [30] He delivers even the one who is not innocent,
>   who will be delivered through the cleanness of your hands."

Again, living close to Christ, being guided constantly by the Spirit, and freely offering forgiveness as a way of life is the absolute opposite of easy. We must remind ourselves we live in a world that is not our home and is hostile toward the things of God. If that were not enough, there are times as we progress in our walk when the Father will test us in order to reveal whether or not we truly have the fullness of God's forgiving nature within us or not. It may be that we will be reminded of past wounds through a simple phone call where a name is mentioned;

LESSON 6:
WHAT IS RECONCILIATION? (PART 2)

it may be that we surprisingly see a past offender at the grocery store or restaurant; it may be that they initiate communication after a long absence through email or a social network message. Whatever the case may be, our emotions will point the way to how we are living. If revenge or anger immediately spring up, then we are not living in God's forgiveness. If we would rather flee the situation rather than stay and be cordial, then we have a ways to go in experiencing the fullness of God's forgiving nature. It matters not what was done to you, the Lord desires everyone to continue processing their wounds toward the truth until we have received the fullness of His forgiveness, which extends naturally to others. If you need to say to yourself over and over, "This is between God and me. It really does not depend upon them at all," go ahead and say it aloud. Injustice and wounds done to you result in that natural response of anger and frustration, which are understandable and allowable. However, God calls us to move toward the offering of forgiveness 100 percent of the time, not based upon what they deserve, but based upon His nature—forgiveness. We will reach the fullness of this forgiveness when we can intercede in prayer on the other party's behalf; when we are able to ask God to shatter their hardness of heart and spirit, so they may be free to live a life of freedom and joy.

At one of our retreats, we had a couple from out of town. Both the husband and the wife had been previously divorced and been married to each other for about 20 years. Thirty or so years earlier, the wife's ex-husband had kidnapped their daughter and moved to another state. The wife at the time did not have the wherewithal to pursue legal remedies and thus lost the ability to have a relationship with her daughter. In recent years, she was able to locate her daughter, now an adult, and made attempts to reconcile the relationship. Her daughter had been poisoned by her father. Because her thoughts about her mother had been horribly tainted by her father, she rebuffed any attempt to even talk together. She specifically requested that her mother leave her alone and never contact her again.

The wife held a deep level of bitterness toward her ex-husband and now toward her daughter who was not unwilling to open up even simple communications. The wife was living under additional pressure of disappointment and resignation (thinking that God was not really good), along with a level of guilt that she did not fight for her daughter when she was kidnapped. There were lots of emotions dominating her soul, resulting in a life of sadness and heaviness. During the retreat we addressed this whole issue of forgiveness and reconciliation: that God calls us to forgive 100 percent of the time and 100 percent of people, including those who have hurt us deeply. The wife recognized that this issue had put her in bondage and was the cause of her deep sadness. She spent time one afternoon in the Scriptures and in the Spirit, allowing God to transform her heart. She fully received His forgiveness and the ability to forgive both her ex-husband

LESSON 6:
WHAT IS RECONCILIATION? (PART 2)

and her daughter. On the last day of the retreat she announced that she had experienced such freedom that she could intercede for both of them, that God would intervene in their lives to reveal to them each His forgiveness and thus a desire to reconcile the relationship of the daughter with her.

During her time of intercession, she heard God speak to her that He would bring about reconciliation with her daughter. The next day we received an incredible phone call. Having returned back home, the wife received a phone call from her daughter telling her that she had recently accepted Christ as Lord and Savior, and though she had struggled with her own issue of forgiveness and was not willing to even talk to her mother, God had broken through on Sunday and helped the daughter understand forgiveness. He gave her a desire to reconcile, that she was to call her mother to set up a time to meet and open the relationship. How cool is that? One of the beautiful truths of God is that He works both sides of every problem. This is one of the reasons we are to simply live in forgiveness, offer reconciliation, and allow God to do His work to bring about His desire for freedom and reconciled relationships. This was certainly a real example to all of us of the power of forgiveness and the beauty of reconciliation through forgiveness and intercession.

With this real story in mind, are there some painful and/or traumatic events in your past? Regardless of your involvement or guilt for lack of involvement, you might be in bondage to your bitterness and guilt just like this woman was. However, through forgiveness and allowing God to transform your heart, you can be released from all of your past hurts, even the excruciating events, and be set free. Are you willing to let God transform you from the inside out as well?

_____
_____
_____
_____
_____
_____
_____
_____
_____
_____
_____

LESSON 6:
WHAT IS RECONCILIATION? (PART 2)

LESSON 7:
AMBASSADORS IN RECONCILIATION

We are called to be ambassadors for Christ in His ministry of reconciliation. Read through these verses and then write how we are called to each.

Read Matthew 5:21-26.

Anger

21 "You have heard that it was said to those of old, 'You shall not murder; and whoever murders will be liable to judgment.' 22 But I say to you that everyone who is angry with his brother[a] will be liable to judgment; whoever insults[b] his brother will be liable to the council; and whoever says, 'You fool!' will be liable to the hell[c] of fire. 23 So if you are offering your gift at the altar and there remember that your brother has something against you, 24 leave your gift there before the altar and go. First be reconciled to your brother, and then come and offer your gift. 25 Come to terms quickly with your accuser while you are going with him to court, lest your accuser hand you over to the judge, and the judge to the guard, and you be put in prison. 26 Truly, I say to you, you will never get out until you have paid the last penny.[d]

"Those who have been reconciled are called, even ordered, to tell those who are not yet of God's flock about His forgiving nature, about His freely offered gift, about how to live in peace with their mighty and loving Creator."

LESSON 7:
AMBASSADORS IN RECONCILIATION

Read 2 Corinthians 5:12-21.

12 We are not commending ourselves to you again but giving you cause to boast about us, so that you may be able to answer those who boast about outward appearance and not about what is in the heart. 13 For if we are beside ourselves, it is for God; if we are in our right mind, it is for you. 14 For the love of Christ controls us, because we have concluded this: that one has died for all, therefore all have died; 15 and he died for all, that those who live might no longer live for themselves but for him who for their sake died and was raised. 16 From now on, therefore, we regard no one according to the flesh. Even though we once regarded Christ according to the flesh, we regard him thus no longer. 17 Therefore, if anyone is in Christ, he is a new creation.[a] The old has passed away; behold, the new has come. 18 All this is from God, who through Christ reconciled us to himself and gave us the ministry of reconciliation; 19 that is, in Christ God was reconciling[b] the world to himself, not counting their trespasses against them, and entrusting to us the message of reconciliation. 20 Therefore, we are ambassadors for Christ, God making his appeal through us. We implore you on behalf of Christ, be reconciled to God. 21 For our sake he made him to be sin who knew no sin, so that in him we might become the righteousness of God.

Read Hebrews 12:12-17.

12 Therefore lift your drooping hands and strengthen your weak knees, 13 and make straight paths for your feet, so that what is lame may not be put out of joint but rather be healed. 14 Strive for peace with everyone, and for the holiness without which no one will see the Lord. 15 See to it that no one fails to obtain the grace of God; that no "root of bitterness" springs up and causes trouble, and by it many become defiled; 16 that no one is sexually immoral or unholy like

LESSON 7:
AMBASSADORS IN RECONCILIATION

> Esau, who sold his birthright for a single meal. [17]For you know that afterward, when he desired to inherit the blessing, he was rejected, for he found no chance to repent, though he sought it with tears.

_____
_____
_____
_____

We have firmly established God's desire to reconcile all people to Himself and His desire for us to show this same behavior to everyone we encounter. Our behavior indeed shows the world how we live and by which kingdom we walk (the kingdom of light or the kingdom of darkness). We are to maintain living in the Spirit by taking to heart everything God has set forth in His Word. We are to cherish the Scriptures and live according to them. We are to flee every appearance of evil and only seek that which is good and profitable. When we live led by God's Spirit, these behaviors are a natural outpouring of a grateful heart by one who truly loves the Lord. God takes care of His own. He is mighty to save, and He will save. He is able to deliver His children, and He will deliver them. He does hear His children's pleas, and He delights in answering them. From thankful hearts and the overflow of gladness, we have a job to do in this dying and hurting world. We are called to be ambassadors for Christ and His ministry of reconciliation. Those who have been reconciled are called, even ordered, to tell those who are not yet of God's flock about His forgiving nature, about His freely offered gift, about how to live in peace with their mighty and loving Creator. Such a mission can only be told by those who have received, and only those who have received can go out with the undying passion and unrelenting fire needed to take the Good News to the world.

Read Romans 12:17-19.

[17] Repay no one evil for evil, but give thought to do what is honorable in the sight of all. [18] If possible, so far as it depends on you, live peaceably with all. [19] Beloved, never avenge yourselves, but leave it[a] to the wrath of God, for it is written, "Vengeance is mine, I will repay, says the Lord."

LESSON 7:
AMBASSADORS IN RECONCILIATION

> **Read Psalm 34:11-22.**
>
> ¹¹ Come, O children, listen to me;
>   I will teach you the fear of the Lord.
> ¹² What man is there who desires life
>   and loves many days, that he may see good?
> ¹³ Keep your tongue from evil
>   and your lips from speaking deceit.
> ¹⁴ Turn away from evil and do good;
>   seek peace and pursue it.
> ¹⁵ The eyes of the Lord are toward the righteous
>   and his ears toward their cry.
> ¹⁶ The face of the Lord is against those who do evil,
>   to cut off the memory of them from the earth.
> ¹⁷ When the righteous cry for help, the Lord hears
>   and delivers them out of all their troubles.
> ¹⁸ The Lord is near to the brokenhearted
>   and saves the crushed in spirit.
> ¹⁹ Many are the afflictions of the righteous,
>   but the Lord delivers him out of them all.
> ²⁰ He keeps all his bones;
>   not one of them is broken.
> ²¹ Affliction will slay the wicked,
>   and those who hate the righteous will be condemned.
> ²² The Lord redeems the life of his servants;
>   none of those who take refuge in him will be condemned.

When we follow Christ, we are called to be His ambassadors. What exactly is an ambassador? It is defined as a diplomatic official of the highest rank, sent by the ruler of a state or country to another state or country as its resident representative or to represent them on a temporary mission. So, God's Word seems to be labeling all believers as God's resident representatives on Earth to execute His desires while we are temporarily living on this Earth. What does God desire His ambassadors to do? Primarily, to offer reconciliation to each and every person we encounter; to show them, to tell them, to beg them to be reconciled to God directly. God deeply desires and longs for all of creation to be reconciled to Him, and when we are walking according to His Spirit, that same desire and longing wells up in each of

LESSON 7:
AMBASSADORS IN RECONCILIATION

us when thinking about our friends, family, and co-workers. Having been told over and over again, we know how to walk in the Spirit: abiding in the Word, abiding in relationship with Jesus, abiding in prayer. It seems pretty simple but remember John 15:5 states how we can do *nothing* apart from Christ. This means God's desire is for others to be reconciled to God as well. We really cannot do anything apart from Him. Reconciliation is not merely resolving an issue between two people or groups. Rather, reconciliation seeks to bring the life of God Almighty into existing relationships in order to bring freedom, joy, peace, awe, and wonder.

As we are being led by the Spirit and are doing our best to be at peace with everyone else, we cannot sacrifice the truth for the sake of peace. In no way are we expected to compromise or give in to others merely to avoid conflict, nor are we expected to allow others to continually hurt us. Instead, the expectation put upon us is to have hearts seeking peace and being willing to work at the issue with the other party until a conclusion, preferably one that leads to full reconciliation and peace, is met. Scripture also states that if we have hurt or done something against another and recognize our error during our worship or prayer time, we are to immediately go to them and process through what was done in order to achieve reconciliation. The motivation here is placed upon the believer to process the truth, confess any and all wrong, and to seek a resolution and restoration. If we are the harmed ones and have legitimate anger and frustration, we are to forgive them first and then follow that with an opportunity to discuss the conflict, process through it, and offer peace and reconciliation with our offender.

How are we to offer reconciliation?

On same basis as He offers it to us. We must stand on truth, process truth, and not move off our understanding of truth until the resolution is satisfactory to our truth. Read through these verses and write out how we are to process our truth with another.

Read Psalm 25:4-5.

⁴ He who has clean hands and a pure heart,
  who does not lift up his soul to what is false
  and does not swear deceitfully.
⁵ He will receive blessing from the Lord
  and righteousness from the God of his salvation.

LESSON 7:
AMBASSADORS IN RECONCILIATION

> **Read Psalm 25:10.**
>
> ¹⁰ All the paths of the Lord are steadfast love and faithfulness,
>   for those who keep his covenant and his testimonies.

> **Read Ephesians 4:11-16; 4:25-27; 4:29-32.**
>
> ¹¹ And he gave the apostles, the prophets, the evangelists, the shepherds[a] and teachers,[b] ¹² to equip the saints for the work of ministry, for building up the body of Christ, ¹³ until we all attain to the unity of the faith and of the knowledge of the Son of God, to mature manhood,[c] to the measure of the stature of the fullness of Christ, ¹⁴ so that we may no longer be children, tossed to and fro by the waves and carried about by every wind of doctrine, by human cunning, by craftiness in deceitful schemes. ¹⁵ Rather, speaking the truth in love, we are to grow up in every way into him who is the head, into Christ, ¹⁶ from whom the whole body, joined and held together by every joint with which it is equipped, when each part is working properly, makes the body grow so that it builds itself up in love.

LESSON 7:
AMBASSADORS IN RECONCILIATION

> 25 Therefore, having put away falsehood, let each one of you speak the truth with his neighbor, for we are members one of another. 26 Be angry and do not sin; do not let the sun go down on your anger, 27 and give no opportunity to the devil.
>
> 29 Let no corrupting talk come out of your mouths, but only such as is good for building up, as fits the occasion, that it may give grace to those who hear. 30 And do not grieve the Holy Spirit of God, by whom you were sealed for the day of redemption. 31 Let all bitterness and wrath and anger and clamor and slander be put away from you, along with all malice. 32 Be kind to one another, tenderhearted, forgiving one another, as God in Christ forgave you.

_____
_____
_____
_____
_____

    We must be willing to adjust our own truth as the other party's truth becomes understood and received (including confessing wrongdoing and injustice if I have contributed to misunderstanding or hurt the other person).

    We also must be willing to adjust our own truth as God's greater truth becomes understood and received.

    Again, how are we to offer reconciliation to others? On the same basis God offers it to us. We must stand on unwavering truth, process through the truth, and refuse to move off our own understanding of truth until the resolution is satisfactory to both parties involved in working toward reconciliation. Where have we heard this before: forgive and love first and then offer reconciliation with God? It reminds us of the cross. So, in the same way Christ offers us forgiveness and reconciliation to the Father through the work done on the cross, we are to offer forgiveness and reconciliation to others. Truth must prevail as we stand firmly rooted on that which has been set forth in God's Word. Processing the hurt and offense done to us is difficult and painful, but we must do so in a way that glorifies God, in truth and love. And we must stay the course until the resolution to the conflict comes and it leads to reconciliation to both parties.

    However, when we truly seek reconciliation with someone who has hurt us, we must be willing to adjust our understanding to their truth. Now, God's truth never changes and in no way are we to change our understanding or mind with anything contrary to what can be found in Scripture. However, our personal truth about what happened within an incident, which includes our perception of intention, what was

LESSON 7:
AMBASSADORS IN RECONCILIATION

said, and how we feel must be adjusted to what the other side says about their perception of intention, reception, words said, and how they felt. We must be willing to understand where they are coming from and receive what they say to us about us, regardless of how much it initially hurts. We must be humble enough to confess to any wrong or injustice done on our part in response to our wound. If we have contributed to the misunderstanding between the two parties or hurt the other side in any way, we must also ask for forgiveness from them.

It is also necessary for us to speak the truth in love. When we approach the conflict with respect and tenderness, the opportunity for reconciliation is genuine. Avoid ignoring the truth for just the appearance of a reconciled relationship. The truth does set us free, and only when the truth is embraced can a real reconciliation occur. Again, regardless of how difficult this may be, we must be willing to stay within this process until a heart-level agreement can be made. Stick with it until you fully understand their side, until the negative emotions subside, until freedom comes. Then and only then can conflict be resolved, forgiveness be offered on both sides, and reconciliation and restoration happen. Now, practically speaking, how is this lived out?

Always begin with the Lord and let His truth guide you into all truth, regardless of the circumstance. From there, we process through the conflict to a resolution.

How does this work in reality?

How does all of this work in everyday life? I will share a situation that illustrates how this works. I received a phone call one day from a senior executive of a Fortune 500 company, whom I knew as an acquaintance. He said that he knew that I could help people process God's will and wanted to meet for lunch to process what he believed he was understanding as God's will. At lunch he proceeded to say that he believed God was calling him out of being an executive to serve as a senior preaching pastor—even though he had no formal seminary education or training. I listened respectfully. Having seen him speak publicly before, I did not sense that his gift was preaching. However, in seeking God's will, it is not to be based on what we sense but rather on what we hear. So, during our conversation, I prayed for God to give me revelation about His will regarding this executive leaving his position to become a pastor. What I heard was "no," it was not His will, but that this executive was seeking his own will. So, after asking a few questions, I simply stated that my Spirit could not confirm that what he was hearing was God's will, and therefore encouraged him to seek further to truly hear God's plan. Knowing that God will communicate His desires directly, I understood that it was, and is, not my right to say that God's will was this or that, but rather share the truth of what I heard and either say yes, my Spirit confirmed that, or no my Spirit did not confirm that.

LESSON 7:
AMBASSADORS IN RECONCILIATION

Since we, as believers, have the same Holy Spirit, it actually is rather easy to come to agreement and confirmation because the Spirit in us will reinforce God's will collectively. Upon me sharing what I was hearing, this person slammed down his utensils, stormed out, and left me to have lunch alone (and pick up the bill). I was surprised but knew that I had been faithful to what I had heard from God. A few days later I received a four-page, hand written letter from this executive, accusing me of being worse than an infidel, that I don't know what I'm doing, that I don't hear God, and that I should stop assisting anyone in attempting to hear God's will. Four pages of vituperative accusations against my character, my Christianity, and my relationship with God! Needless to say, I was angry and hurt. This person had called me, I did not say directly that I disagreed with his understanding of God's will but just suggested that he consider going further. His character assassination on me was inappropriate and certainly not deserved. I sat down and began to write a rebuttal and defense to his accusations. My emotions were high, and I realized that I had un-forgiveness toward this person.

But I also know that, first and foremost, we all must go to forgiveness.

> **Read Psalm 4:4-5.**
>
> 4 Be angry,[a] and do not sin;
>   ponder in your own hearts on your beds, and be silent. Selah
> 5 Offer right sacrifices,
>   and put your trust in the Lord.

_____
_____
_____
_____
_____

> **Read Ephesians 4:32.**
>
> 32 Be kind to one another, tenderhearted, forgiving one another, as God in Christ forgave you.

LESSON 7:
AMBASSADORS IN RECONCILIATION

_____
_____
_____
_____
_____

The other party deserved my anger and separation. But based upon receiving the nature of God and what He has done on behalf of us all, especially me, I knew anger and separation were not options.

Read Ephesians 4:26-27.

[26] Be angry and do not sin; do not let the sun go down on your anger, [27] and give no opportunity to the devil.

Read Luke 11:2-4.

[2] And he said to them, "When you pray, say:
"Father, hallowed be your name.
Your kingdom come.
[3] Give us each day our daily bread,[a]
[4] and forgive us our sins,
  for we ourselves forgive everyone who is indebted to us.
And lead us not into temptation."

Nothing has changed with what has been said. Forgiveness from God is never based upon what we deserve. Neither should we offer forgiveness to others based upon what they deserve. Our anger and subsequent separation from the one(s) who hurt us want to hold on to the animosity and unforgiveness, but we must not give in to their enticing message. We offer forgiveness based upon what God has done on our behalf already, based upon God's nature we have experienced. Forgiving others is to our benefit and necessary to live truly free. The forgiven shall forgive. And not just at an intellectual level, but at the deepest heart level. It is at this level where the very Spirit of God resides and allows us to fully and gratefully appreciate our own forgiveness and thus translate that thankfulness into freely forgiving others.

LESSON 7:
AMBASSADORS IN RECONCILIATION

In the situation with this executive, I first had to go off into communion with the Father to resettle my heart and to receive His nature in me about this person: for me to have true forgiveness on the same basis that God gave me and not what this person deserved. What he deserved was to get my anger and wrath and for me to "get him back." However, since forgiveness is between me and God, I had to get my heart back to forgiveness so that I could truly have freedom and the reality of forgiveness in my heart for this person—not as an intellectual step of obedience, but a true forgiveness in my heart.

Second, we must move toward forgiveness with respect, kindness, honor:

> **Philippians 2:1-11.**
>
> **Christ's Example of Humility**
> **2** So if there is any encouragement in Christ, any comfort from love, any participation in the Spirit, any affection and sympathy, ² complete my joy by being of the same mind, having the same love, being in full accord and of one mind. ³ Do nothing from selfish ambition or conceit, but in humility count others more significant than yourselves. ⁴ Let each of you look not only to his own interests, but also to the interests of others. ⁵ Have this mind among yourselves, which is yours in Christ Jesus,[a] ⁶ who, though he was in the form of God, did not count equality with God a thing to be grasped,[b] ⁷ but emptied himself, by taking the form of a servant,[c] being born in the likeness of men. ⁸ And being found in human form, he humbled himself by becoming obedient to the point of death, even death on a cross. ⁹ Therefore God has highly exalted him and bestowed on him the name that is above every name, ¹⁰ so that at the name of Jesus every knee should bow, in heaven and on earth and under the earth, ¹¹ and every tongue confess that Jesus Christ is Lord, to the glory of God the Father.

_____
_____
_____
_____
_____

LESSON 7:
AMBASSADORS IN RECONCILIATION

> **Re-read Ephesians 4:25-32.**
>
> ²⁵ Therefore, having put away falsehood, let each one of you speak the truth with his neighbor, for we are members one of another. ²⁶ Be angry and do not sin; do not let the sun go down on your anger, ²⁷ and give no opportunity to the devil. ²⁸ Let the thief no longer steal, but rather let him labor, doing honest work with his own hands, so that he may have something to share with anyone in need. ²⁹ Let no corrupting talk come out of your mouths, but only such as is good for building up, as fits the occasion, that it may give grace to those who hear. ³⁰ And do not grieve the Holy Spirit of God, by whom you were sealed for the day of redemption. ³¹ Let all bitterness and wrath and anger and clamor and slander be put away from you, along with all malice. ³² Be kind to one another, tenderhearted, forgiving one another, as God in Christ forgave you.

_____
_____
_____
_____
_____

If you find you are still emotionally angry and seeking revenge, this means you are not in forgiveness and are not able, in peace and freedom, to process the truth needed for reconciliation.

If this is the case, then reevaluate:

- How does each see the truth about this situation?
- What resolutions does each have about this situation?
- Is there a resolution satisfactory to each party? Why or why not?

Scripture tells us our emotions toward everyone should be honoring, respectful, and kind, even and especially to those with whom there is conflict. When these emotions marry the truth, people see God living in us. Our goal is not to just bring about a solution that everyone agrees to and accepts. More

LESSON 7:
AMBASSADORS IN RECONCILIATION

importantly, it is to show people and help them realize how walking in the Spirit is a place of immense peace and joy, a place of righteousness, a place of ultimate freedom and wonder. How we offer and discuss reconciliation directly reflects Christ's nature within us and our opposing party will see that beauty and freedom we have embraced and offer to them in turn. However, if we continue to experience emotions of anger or revenge toward another, it simply means we have not forgiven them and are not able to walk in peace and freedom yet. As noted above, when this is the case, we need to ask ourselves some basic questions:

- How does each party see the truth about the situation at hand?
- What resolutions does each side offer regarding this situation?
- Is there a resolution which satisfies each party?
- If so, great! If not, why or why not?

In my example with this executive, having forgiveness in my heart, I was able to call him and say that I received his letter and that I would like to meet again to discuss it all. Because I had forgiveness, I could treat him with honor and respect, even in my request to meet.

At this point, the result is usually clear. Typically, the parties involved have either:

- processed the truth of the situation until there is agreement on the resolution so that reconciliation and a restored relationship ensues
- attempted to process the truth of the situation that cannot reach agreement on the resolution and remained either partially or completely un-reconciled
- they are not willing to process the truth at all and remained completely un-reconciled

When there is an attempt to process truth, but the opposing sides still see things differently and as of yet, there is no resolution making everyone happy, the best action is to temporarily separate and return to your bed—time alone (Psalm 4:4-5) and process with the Lord. Continue praying and seeking His voice, forgiveness, and wisdom until you have reestablished true forgiveness in your own heart. Only then do you return to process truth with the other person(s) with respect and tenderness. If a resolution still cannot be made, we need to continue to stay in forgiveness and ask the Father to provide resolution to the situation and

LESSON 7:
AMBASSADORS IN RECONCILIATION

conflict. If both parties are walking in the Spirit and know that God will provide a solution, they can continue to respect and honor each other as they seek to work through truth until a resolution is reached. Forgiveness will characterize each of their hearts along with a respectful desire to get to God's truth knowing that God's truth will become known, and then full reconciliation can be reached.

The result will be clear:

Either you agree to be restored and reconciled, or you do not agree (still see things differently and no discussed resolution is satisfactory to either party), in which case there are three possibilities to come to reconciliation:

- My resolution is truth, and God has to change the other party's heart to understand and receive that truth.

- The other party's resolution is truth, and God has to change my heart to understand and receive that truth.

- God reveals a new resolution as He changes both parties' hearts to understand and receive this new truth.

This may take time, which is okay, as long as:

- We both are living in forgiveness.

- We have listened, acknowledged, and clarified each other's view of truth.

- We continue to act with respect, kindness, and honor toward each other.

- Our lack of agreement does not ruin our day, our night, our weekend. We are able to set it aside and come back to it as we stay with it until agreement comes.

When we are both living in forgiveness, we understand that one of these possibilities will be revealed to us by God. And since both of us are in humility seeking God's will, we are willing to let God change our heart, change the other person's heart, or show us something brand new that brings about the answer to reconciliation. This is why it is so easy to stay in the place of forgiveness with a heart toward reconciliation, including that my position and my understanding that truth may need to be altered and changed by God to get to the real truth and thus real reconciliation.

Linda and I owned an investment property that had provided stable cash flow for our portfolio. I had come to the conclusion that it would be a good idea to sell

LESSON 7:
AMBASSADORS IN RECONCILIATION

the property and invest in another property. Linda disagreed and did not sense that this was God's will. I felt strongly, and so I worked hard to persuade her that this was a good idea. She felt equally as strongly and resisted. We got into a debate and were at odds with each other. Understanding the process of forgiveness and reconciliation, we went to our own spaces and got our hearts right with God. As we received forgiveness toward each other, (again on the same basis that He forgive us, through His nature, and not what we deserved), we were then able to come back together and begin processing the truth about what each of us felt about this situation. (The tools we use are described below.) We both still had strength of conviction and did not reach resolution. However, because we were in forgiveness, we could respect and honor each other and know God would give us His resolution. We were able to enjoy the day and the weekend following without allowing this disagreement to burden us.

We both then went to prayer knowing that God would either change my heart, Linda's heart, or show us something new. Over the following week, God showed me that my conclusions were not in sync with His and that the timing for selling this investment property was not to be now. Through a willingness to humbly seek God's will, He changed my heart, and I was willing to accept His answer. I then went to Linda and explained that God had changed my mind, and that it was not time to sell, as she had heard. We reached resolution and were fully reconciled. Interesting enough, a year later the Lord showed us both that the timing was right for the sale of the property—and it sold at full price in a very depressed market! We both would like to testify that this process is really not difficult, that as we processed through our differences (which were significant), we were able to get to and stay in joy, as seeking and receiving God's will is best, and there is nothing better.

So, what is required for all this to work?

- Each party must first go to and remain in forgiveness.

- Each party must have a desire to be an ambassador for Christ and have a ministry of reconciliation.

- Each party must be willing to process truth—and have integrity about that truth.

- Each party must be willing to stay with the process until both an agreement and resolution become satisfactory to both.

LESSON 7:
AMBASSADORS IN RECONCILIATION

- Now, if I am in forgiveness and fully willing for all this to work, the other party will set the level of reconciliation depending on their living in forgiveness and willingness to process truth. If there is:

- None, we will not be reconciled at all, and there will be no relationship, and will have separated.

- Partial, there will be a limited processing of truth, but an unwillingness to go to depth of the feelings of hurt experienced by me and see that what they have done has hurt and is unhealthy. At this, we cannot get to a full discussion of a resolution that is satisfactory to me since we never get to processing the full truth. This will result in a surface relationship, we will spend limited time together, and we will have boundaries regarding how much time and in what situations are satisfactory to and healthy for me.

- Complete, we will enjoy a fully restored relationship, with all the benefits of God's forgiveness.

- In order to process together to reach a resolution and reconciliation, the following tools are recommended:

- How does each side see the truth about this situation? A good technique to use for this is to have each side share his/her view of what happened. After they have spoken, repeat what they have said and then ask, "Did I understand you correctly?" and "Is there anything else you would like to say regarding the issue?" Return to the beginning and repeat as many times as needed until both questions are answered positively, then reverse roles until you feel as though you have been fully heard and understood.

- Focus on the actual issue at hand. Once both sides have been fully heard and understood, often what happens is each party realizes they agree on more than they originally thought. Usually there is only one or two key issues needing to be resolved in the conflict. When you realize the actual issues, focus on those alone and work toward a resolution which will bring about reconciliation.

- Offer a solution. Once the key issues have been realized and discussed, each side should take a turn in offering a resolution satisfactory to both parties.

LESSON 7:
AMBASSADORS IN RECONCILIATION

First, the resolution would be stated and why it would be reasonable. Next, they would explain what they are willing to do (or not do, whatever the case may be) to resolve the issue. Then the opposing party would ask the same questions as before regarding the resolution, "Did I understand you correctly?" and "Is there anything else you would like to say here?" Once they are both positive answers, the other person takes a turn, just as before.

- Discuss if the solutions are acceptable to everyone. If they are, fantastic! Agree on the solution and live in the freedom of a reconciled and fully restored relationship, agreeing to not bring up the conflict again in the future. However, if neither resolution is adequate, more work needs to be done. Remember, the solution to the problem cannot violate Christ's truth. Therefore, the solutions must be truthful, and if they are not, then continue the process until they are. If a truthful resolution cannot be agreed upon, you must be willing to not be reconciled.

- The sooner we choose to process the truth, forgive, come to a resolution, and continue down the path toward full reconciliation, the sooner we will reap the benefits of walking in the Spirit: peace that passes all understanding and the freedom that truly sets us free. However, going through the entire process may take some time, which is completely understandable and acceptable. Our role is to make sure that we are living in forgiveness and let God speak to the other side.

Also, make sure you are listening to the other party's side, clarifying along the way as needed, all the while acknowledging their feelings and words and view of the truth. In addition, ensure to continue acting with respect, kindness, and honor toward our offender. However, if you are not being treated with respect and honor, the process may have to cease until respect can be shown on both sides or both parties will have to live unreconciled. If this is being threatened, ask yourself and your offender if you both can set aside the conflict until a later date, but with a continued heart toward resolution. With these attitudes and guidelines practiced, we should be able to live in such a way that a lack of agreement does not ruin our attitudes, our days and nights, our interactions with others. For this to work fully, a few things must happen on both sides of the conflict:

- Each party must turn first to forgiveness and remain in forgiveness. If you are operating in forgiveness but your offender is not, keep the forgiving mindset. If believers continue to walk guided by the Spirit and remain humble, it creates an environment where it is easier for the other party to process with respect, kindness, and honor.

LESSON 7:
AMBASSADORS IN RECONCILIATION

- Each party must have a desire to be an ambassador for Christ and have a ministry of reconciliation. Again, we are only responsible for ourselves. If the opposing person or party has no desire to participate in the ministry of reconciliation, we are to remain being ambassadors and continue treating them with respect. The offer to process through the conflict is presented over and over with respect. Each party must be willing to process the truth of the situation and have integrity while doing it.

- Each party must be willing to process truth—and have integrity about that truth. You need to continually stand on the truth, share the truth, and never compromise the truth. Just as important is for you to ask the other person(s) to stand on their truth, share their truth, and not compromise their truth. Why? You do not want the other party to give in or cave merely for the sake of resolving or avoiding conflict. When this happens, conflicts are never resolved. Because of this, you need to create a safe environment for them to continue to share what's on their heart so that a resolution based around truth is truly reached. This is particularly significant for a couple where one party generally will give in just to avoid the conflict. Work hard at this, and you will see the ability to process truth well will lead to wonderful resolutions and the fulfillment of God's will.

- Each party must be willing to stay within the process until an agreement is found and a resolution suitable for both parties is decided. As far as it concerns you, you should always be willing to continue the reconciliation process. The other party, due to their lack of forgiveness and bondage to their own soul wounds, may walk away from the process and refuse to process further. Remember, your call is to forgive at all times but that reconciliation is based upon truth. You cannot control the other party's response to that truth. So, if they are not willing to be reconciled, then you have to be willing to let the relationship be unreconciled but always having the freedom in forgiveness and a willingness to process again if the other party ever decides they desire to pursue truth with you.

Each and every step happens and happens seamlessly in an ideal situation. But, we do not always find ourselves in ideal situations. However, less-than-perfect circumstances do not negate how we are to act toward the other person. We are responsible for our own actions, reactions, and responses. If you and I walk in forgiveness and are fully willing to work out the conflict, the opposing side decides upon the future of the relationship. They set the level of reconciliation based upon

LESSON 7:
AMBASSADORS IN RECONCILIATION

how they walk, if they are going to live in forgiveness or not. If they choose to withhold forgiveness completely, there will be no reconciliation. The relationship has been severed, and a separation will take place between the two. Some people decide to only partially forgive. In these circumstances, they will process the truth and hurt in a limited fashion. They refuse to plunge the depths of the hurt feelings experienced by both sides and will continue to live so unhealthily. Their refusal to fully process the conflict will result in lack of resolution satisfactory to both sides since truth is not completely addressed. What typically happens here is that the relationship will continue only at a surface level, and any time spent between the two of you will be rather limited. There will be new noticeable boundaries in place regarding how much time and in what circumstances are comfortable and healthy.

In my example with the executive, upon me making a phone call to offer an opportunity to sit and process what happened between us, the executive shouted that he never wanted to talk to me again and hung up. Having already gone to forgiveness, I remained in forgiveness. Knowing that it takes two parties to reach reconciliation through processing truth together, and having offered to sit and process the truth, I knew that there was nothing more for me to do. I did not let this burden me or cause me to develop any roots of bitterness. In fact, I gave no thought about it, except as I was reminded by God to intercede for this individual. I periodically saw him at a distance and had no trouble being in the same room with him, saying a friendly hello and asking how he was doing. His answers were always short, and he wanted to quickly depart from being with me. I understood that his anger and un-forgiveness were actually trapping him and could actually feel sorry for what had occurred within his soul, which is why I could go to intercession on his behalf. I could neither force him to process with me, nor could I dismiss the truth just for the sake of apparent reconciliation. I was called to carry out what Christ has carried out—complete forgiveness based upon His nature, and then an offer of reconciliation—understanding that reconciliation may not be possible because of the inability to process truth.

As we serve as ambassadors in this ministry of reconciliation, we and the other party experience wonderful benefits:

- Redemption (we receive life back)
- His righteousness
- Guidance
- Joy
- He forgets our failure
- Spiritual power and authority
- Peace

LESSON 7:
AMBASSADORS IN RECONCILIATION

- Mercy, kindness, and tenderness
- Healing
- Restoration from destructive patterns
- Satisfaction with good things (renewal)

In my example with the executive, nearly a year went by. I had not experienced any anger or bitterness toward him, nor was I burdened by our break in the relationship. I was living in forgiveness and was willing to process truth through to reconciliation, even though he was not. Then one day I received a phone call from him. He said that he would like to meet me for lunch and talk. Having been in forgiveness, I immediately agreed. This is one of the beauties of forgiveness: When the other party who hurt us decides to process the truth, we are always prepared to join the process, with no anger or bitterness coming with us into the process. At lunch, he began with saying he was sorry for what had transpired between us; that he had tried for over a year to become a pastor; that God had blocked every attempt and now he realized he had been seeking his own will and was not really interested in God's will. Looking back, he also realized I had been hearing from God and that it was my role as one of God's holy priesthood, to communicate what I was hearing and not to compromise what I was hearing. He admitted that his response was inappropriate and cruel. I shared what I had felt both at the beginning of the process (anger and hurt) and throughout the process (forgiveness and intercession), but that I felt no ill will toward him and was thrilled that he had come to know God's will and was now prepared to follow what God had in mind for his life. We both let it all go and were fully reconciled to a positive and healthy relationship. Since that time, he has been called, as an executive, to reach and train churches in amazing recovery ministries and is truly serving as a minister of God, in a role designed for him by God to expand what was on God's heart for the Kingdom.

Throughout this book we have asked you to address some painful issues in your own life, past hurts, past disappointments, traumas, etc., and gently lead you into the truth of the freedom and love and full life available to you. By now, you have all of the tools and resources to live in forgiveness yourself. You have the ability to offer reconciliation to anyone, regardless of what they have done or may do to you in the future. Remember, you cannot do anything apart from Christ, apart from walking in His Spirit, apart from Him abiding in you as you abide in Him. The choice to live in freedom and in love is always contingent upon you, because God's work has already been accomplished upon the cross—once and for all.

As you allow the Holy Spirit to transform your mind, your heart, your life, you will greatly reap all of the benefits of living in the Kingdom and that life will

LESSON 7:
AMBASSADORS IN RECONCILIATION

be everything you have ever wanted, dared to dream of, and more. The choice is yours, and the call to follow Christ in forgiveness and reconciliation is always available to you. Leave behind your past failures, your former pain, and look forward and upward. The questions asked to you from your Heavenly Father are simply and always this:

Why not today? Why not now?

Write down what you have learned about the truths of forgiveness and reconciliation, and the implications for us to be reconciled with God and for us to reconcile with others.

_____
_____
_____
_____
_____
_____
_____
_____
_____
_____
_____
_____
_____
_____
_____
_____
_____
_____
_____
_____
_____
_____
_____
_____

LESSON 7:
AMBASSADORS IN RECONCILIATION

LESSON 8:
PRACTICAL WAYS OF RECONCILIATION IN A VARIETY OF SITUATIONS

> "When we pray for non-believers to respond to God's truth, which offers eternal redemption and restoration, we are near the very heart of God."

Work through the following situations that impact our ability to reconcile. Review the verses and write out what they are speaking to you.

1. What about justice? Does the other party deserve justice when in fact, they did wrong and were completely unfair, their deed being a true injustice?

Re-read Romans 12:9-21.

Marks of the True Christian
9 Let love be genuine. Abhor what is evil; hold fast to what is good. 10 Love one another with brotherly affection. Outdo one another in showing honor. 11 Do not be slothful in zeal, be fervent in spirit,[a] serve the Lord. 12 Rejoice in hope, be patient in tribulation, be constant in prayer. 13 Contribute to the needs of the saints and seek to show hospitality.

14 Bless those who persecute you; bless and do not curse them. 15 Rejoice with those who rejoice, weep with those who weep. 16 Live in harmony with one another. Do not be haughty, but associate with the lowly.[b] Never be wise in your own sight. 17 Repay no one evil for evil, but give thought to do what is honorable in the sight of all. 18 If possible, so far as it depends on you, live peaceably with all. 19 Beloved, never avenge yourselves, but leave it[c] to the wrath of God, for it is written, "Vengeance is mine, I will repay, says the Lord." 20 To the contrary, "if your enemy is hungry, feed him; if he is thirsty, give him something to drink; for by so doing you will heap burning coals on his head." 21 Do not be overcome by evil, but overcome evil with good.

_____
_____
_____
_____
_____

LESSON 8:
PRACTICAL WAYS OF RECONCILIATION IN A VARIETY OF SITUATIONS

These verses call us toward:

- Forgiveness

- Kindness, respect, honor

- Replacing good for evil

- Believing that the injustice will be corrected. Justice will prevail; and revenge is up to God to fulfill (have to have long view of it), not me. I can let it go.

Doesn't the other party who did something completely unfair and wrong—a true injustice—need to be set straight and punished?

Again, we are to act contrarily to the rest of the world. We are to be ruled by God's Spirit, by forgiveness. If we constantly have in the forefront of our minds how much we have been forgiven and how much we deserve nothing but God's wrath, we will more readily offer forgiveness to those who hurt us. It is a choice. We must choose to live in and live out forgiveness. We are told to honor, respect, and be kind to those who are evil to us. Romans tells us to repay evil with good. This is impossible to do apart from God living within us, but within this difficulty, we must still choose to believe that injustice will be corrected. God always delivers justice, for He is just and perfectly righteous. His justice will prevail, His justice will be perfect, and it is God's prerogative to exact revenge in His way and in His time.

But, as we walk in the Spirit and understand the truth of justice, we actually are given a different perspective. Instead of us seeking judgment, we have to have a heart for those to see justice and the truth of God that would lead them to repentance and their own walk led by Spirit. When we intercede on behalf of lost ones, we are repaying good for evil. We are praying that their hearts would be made new, that the carnal nature and hard hearts would be replaced with life abundant and tenderness only available through Christ. When we pray for non-believers to respond to God's truth, which offers eternal redemption and restoration, we are near the very heart of God.

For example, our son and his wife, who have two boys, experienced a very scary situation. One of the employees of my son's company was terminated for cause by his supervisor. That person found out where my son lived and came to his house demanding to speak to my son. His wife answered the door and said he was not home and to please leave. This disgruntled employee forced his way a second time, where she and her two boys were, threatening to harm them because he had been let go. Upon learning this, my son called the local police and was able to secure an injunction against this person ever coming into their home and contacting them at all. Unfortunately, this person violated this injunction and sent numerous threatening letters, which my son and his wife ignored. They were worried, fearful, and very angry, and as believers, attempting to not let this burden their lives.

LESSON 8:
PRACTICAL WAYS OF RECONCILIATION IN A VARIETY OF SITUATIONS

However, they both admitted that they had not come to a place of true forgiveness. Then they received a letter stating this former employee had a gun and was going to carry out what was necessary to appease what had happened to him. My son took the letter to the police who then arrested the individual and set a court date for him to appear before the judge. The prosecutor contacted my son and told him they would carry out within the law any sentence that my son recommended. At first my son wanted justice to be served, and he and his wife wanted the court to deliver the longest sentence possible. Nevertheless, we gathered together in what we call "Family Council," and discussed the situation. We first processed whether or not my son and his wife had gone to forgiveness. They had not. We told them before we all could come to God's solution, the necessary first step was to spend time with God until they had reached forgiveness. They did spend the time, and both received forgiveness toward this person.

Then we spent time in looking at justice, and what God had to say about justice in Romans 12:9-20. It was clear that it was not our duty to establish justice but to let God have His own vengeance, for "thus saith" the Lord. Since this person was married and responsible for his wife, my son and wife decided before the Lord to recommend probation with a clear understanding that another violation would result in jail time. My son went even further and paid for the court cost of the second injunction. My son and his wife have not been burdened nor scared any further and since that time have had no threats or contact from this person. They fully understand justice will be served, but that it is up to God fulfilling His call to justice. They understood that they needed to let go of any desire to set things straight on their own. This is a very valuable lesson to all of us about the process of forgiveness and allowing God to deal with justice.

2. What about those who have passed away with no chance for reconciliation?

Read Isaiah 61:1-4; Psalm 103:1-5.

The Year of the Lord's Favor
61 The Spirit of the Lord God is upon me,
    because the Lord has anointed me
to bring good news to the poor;[a]
    he has sent me to bind up the brokenhearted,
to proclaim liberty to the captives,
    and the opening of the prison to those who are bound;[b]
² to proclaim the year of the Lord's favor,

LESSON 8:
PRACTICAL WAYS OF RECONCILIATION IN A VARIETY OF SITUATIONS

> and the day of vengeance of our God;
> to comfort all who mourn;
> ³ to grant to those who mourn in Zion—
> to give them a beautiful headdress instead of ashes,
> the oil of gladness instead of mourning,
> the garment of praise instead of a faint spirit;
> that they may be called oaks of righteousness,
> the planting of the Lord, that he may be glorified.[c]
> ⁴ They shall build up the ancient ruins;
> they shall raise up the former devastations;
> they shall repair the ruined cities,
> the devastations of many generations.

> **Bless the Lord, O My Soul**
>
> Of David.
> **103** Bless the Lord, O my soul,
> and all that is within me,
> bless his holy name!
> ² Bless the Lord, O my soul,
> and forget not all his benefits,
> ³ who forgives all your iniquity,
> who heals all your diseases,
> ⁴ who redeems your life from the pit,
> who crowns you with steadfast love and mercy,
> ⁵ who satisfies you with good
> so that your youth is renewed like the eagle's.

_____
_____
_____
_____

- Understand that forgiveness brings healing, freedom, and release.

LESSON 8:
PRACTICAL WAYS OF RECONCILIATION IN A VARIETY OF SITUATIONS

We still need to process through all of the steps. So, we are to do everything that is within us to forgive and let that forgiveness lead to our healing and the eventual freedom and release from all the hurt. Remember, forgiveness is between you and God and not you and the other party. Even if the other party is deceased, we can still work through to forgiveness for all the hurt and pain that they have cost us. When we reach that level of forgiveness, God then brings us freedom and release from our maintained bondage of anger and bitterness toward the person who is deceased. We can truly let it go and move on to the high calling of Christ Jesus into the beautiful, abundant life He has planned for us. There is nothing more wonderful than being released from the bondage that has captured us for so many years.

In our retreats, Linda and I have seen this over and over again, particularly concerning dead parents and siblings. Often parents have abused, abandoned, rejected, or oppressed their children and then died. Their estranged children are left to deal with the un-forgiveness, anger, and un-reconciliation of that relationship. When the children (who are attending our retreats) received the truth that they can gain freedom from this, they spend time with their Heavenly Father until they receive and experience this forgiveness. They then continue on their journey to have the ability to forgive their dead parents or siblings, knowing that the relationship cannot be reconciled, but that the freedom from the burden of the relationship can be realized. It is a wonderful thing to see the yoke being lifted when they reach this beautiful state of forgiveness and freedom.

3. What about the mother and/or father who have deeply abused or hurt me; and who my still be hurting me?

   - Remember forgiveness

   - Remember the command to honor that comes with a promise of blessing or curse.

Read Exodus 20:12; Ephesians 6:2.

[12] "Honor your father and your mother, that your days may be long in the land that the Lord your God is giving you.

[2] "Honor your father and mother" (this is the first commandment with a promise).

LESSON 8:
PRACTICAL WAYS OF RECONCILIATION IN A VARIETY OF SITUATIONS

_____
_____
_____
_____
_____

How? Though they may not be willing to process any truth, our role is to move the level of reconciliation from none to partial. Here you are to:

- Be willing to have a surface relationship

- Offer respect, kindness, honor

- Establish healthy boundaries while maintaining honor;

    - Pray for protection of heart

    - Practice avoiding getting drawn into unhealthy situations and responding when buttons are pushed

    - If limited time, remember it is for a short time and can be released.

This one is always a very difficult one to process. Our father and mother often have and may continue to hurt and oppress us. Often, they use manipulation and/or guilt to achieve their own personal goals with no thought of the impact or emotional scarring it causes in their children's lives. However, God has commanded us to honor our father and mother and the commandment carries with it the promise of a blessing or a curse.

> **Read Deuteronomy 30:15-20.**
>
> [15] "See, I have set before you today life and good, death and evil. [16] If you obey the commandments of the Lord your God[a] that I command you today, by loving the Lord your God, by walking in his ways, and by keeping his commandments and his statutes and his rules,[b] then you shall live and multiply, and the Lord your God will bless you in the land that you are entering to take possession of it. [17] But if your heart turns away, and you will not hear, but are drawn away to worship other gods and serve them, [18] I declare to you today, that you shall surely perish. You shall not live long in the land that you

LESSON 8:
PRACTICAL WAYS OF RECONCILIATION IN A VARIETY OF SITUATIONS

> are going over the Jordan to enter and possess. [19] I call heaven and earth to witness against you today, that I have set before you life and death, blessing and curse. Therefore, choose life, that you and your offspring may live, [20] loving the Lord your God, obeying his voice and holding fast to him, for he is your life and length of days, that you may dwell in the land that the Lord swore to your fathers, to Abraham, to Isaac, and to Jacob, to give them."

How does this happen? One step at a time and by understanding we have to learn how to process the truth of reconciliation with the joint command of honoring our father and mother. With other people who are not willing to process to reconciliation, we are actually called to dust off our feet and move forward. However, with fathers and mothers we do not have that option. Thus, the key, as with all of our relationships, is to forgive and release the burden of all the hurts and pain that parents have caused us. Although your mother and/or father may not be willing to process any truth, we are still required to do everything in our power to move the parent/child relationship level of reconciliation from severed to partial. We may have to be resigned to the fact to only have a surface relationship with them, which may be extremely difficult. We are to show nothing but respect, kindness, and honor to our parent(s), as commanded by God. And while maintaining honor, establish firm and healthy boundaries with them. Such boundaries are done by:

- Praying for the protection of our heart

- Practicing avoidance when it comes to getting drawn into unhealthy situations

- Avoiding response when our "hot buttons" are pushed

- Remind yourself that it is only for a short time (if there is a time limit), and the release will come when the time is over.

According to Scriptures, we are not allowed a complete separation from our parents. However, we are able to have a minimal or partial relationship that moves toward a complete reconciliation if they are willing to process truth. Yet, parents are often not willing to process truth. Sometimes if we attempt to process truth it makes the situation even worse. Therefore, we are to work at creating times when we can spend time with our parents in that surface-level relationship and not

LESSON 8:
PRACTICAL WAYS OF RECONCILIATION IN A VARIETY OF SITUATIONS

deal with anything deep or heavy. When they attempt to control or manipulate us, we can just let it roll off our backs and not engage in unhealthy dynamics. At the same time, we are not to subject ourselves to situations that only bring about more hurt. There will be times when we will have to say no to various opportunities to be together and then come up with alternative solutions. For example, instead of joining your parents for a holiday, like Christmas, you can choose to enjoy your holiday with your immediate family and offer alternative dates to get together and celebrate differently with your parents. Do not take the command to honor your father and mother as a license for your parents to control or manipulate you. Instead, you are to find that place where you can respect and honor them, be with them, spend enjoyable time with them, and not allow the way they hurt you to impact your heart any further.

In the situation that I described at the beginning of the book about my anger and un-forgiveness toward my mother, I was able to process through to forgiveness and a modest level of a reconciled relationship with my mother. Because she was unwilling to deal with the abuse and dominance of attempting to control me, my wife Linda, and her family, we had to establish boundaries that were healthy for us while giving respect and honor to my mother. Because holidays were of such importance to our immediate family, we no longer were willing to spend the holidays with my mother. What we did do is establish other weekends where Linda and I would spend time with my mother and her husband (not my father, since they were divorced after Linda and I were married). We were respectful and honorable, not reacting to her continued abuse and control, and worked toward just enjoying our time together. As children, we are called to bring honor to our parents, but this can be done in ways that do not allow them to continue to abuse or manipulate us at the same time. Another boundary that we understood was how my mother did not do well in large family meetings. Therefore, we no longer joined in any large group family gatherings, but rather only in small gatherings with my mother and her husband and possibly another of our siblings. This facilitated a more enjoyable experience and did not create the pressure that caused my mother to overreact and dominate. We came to these boundaries through processing together as a couple before God and praying until we reached agreement as to God's will—which is always to honor our parents, while at the same time not allowing them to continue to hurt us in unhealthy ways for us or our children. It worked well, and in the latter days of my mother's life, it actually became sweeter and sweeter.

LESSON 8:
PRACTICAL WAYS OF RECONCILIATION IN A VARIETY OF SITUATIONS

4. What about a person who has cut me off?

Read John 6:53-67; Luke 18:18-30.

53 So Jesus said to them, "Truly, truly, I say to you, unless you eat the flesh of the Son of Man and drink his blood, you have no life in you. 54 Whoever feeds on my flesh and drinks my blood has eternal life, and I will raise him up on the last day. 55 For my flesh is true food, and my blood is true drink. 56 Whoever feeds on my flesh and drinks my blood abides in me, and I in him. 57 As the living Father sent me, and I live because of the Father, so whoever feeds on me, he also will live because of me. 58 This is the bread that came down from heaven, not like the bread[a] the fathers ate, and died. Whoever feeds on this bread will live forever." 59 Jesus[b] said these things in the synagogue, as he taught at Capernaum.

The Words of Eternal Life
60 When many of his disciples heard it, they said, "This is a hard saying; who can listen to it?" 61 But Jesus, knowing in himself that his disciples were grumbling about this, said to them, "Do you take offense at this? 62 Then what if you were to see the Son of Man ascending to where he was before? 63 It is the Spirit who gives life; the flesh is no help at all. The words that I have spoken to you are spirit and life. 64 But there are some of you who do not believe."(For Jesus knew from the beginning who those were who did not believe, and who it was who would betray him.) 65 And he said, "This is why I told you that no one can come to me unless it is granted him by the Father."

66 After this many of his disciples turned back and no longer walked with him. 67 So Jesus said to the twelve, "Do you want to go away as well?"

The Rich Ruler
18 And a ruler asked him, "Good Teacher, what must I do to inherit eternal life?" 19 And Jesus said to him, "Why do you call me good? No one is good except God alone. 20 You know the commandments: 'Do not commit adultery, Do not murder, Do not steal, Do not bear false witness, Honor your father and mother.'" 21 And he said, "All these I have kept from my youth." 22 When Jesus heard this, he said to him, "One thing you still lack. Sell all that you have and distribute to the poor, and you will have treasure in heaven; and come,

LESSON 8:
PRACTICAL WAYS OF RECONCILIATION IN A VARIETY OF SITUATIONS

> follow me."²³ But when he heard these things, he became very sad, for he was extremely rich. ²⁴ Jesus, seeing that he had become sad, said, "How difficult it is for those who have wealth to enter the kingdom of God! ²⁵ For it is easier for a camel to go through the eye of a needle than for a rich person to enter the kingdom of God." ²⁶ Those who heard it said, "Then who can be saved?" ²⁷ But he said, "What is impossible with man is possible with God." ²⁸ And Peter said, "See, we have left our homes and followed you." ²⁹ And he said to them, "Truly, I say to you, there is no one who has left house or wife or brothers[a] or parents or children, for the sake of the kingdom of God, ³⁰ who will not receive many times more in this time, and in the age to come eternal life."

_____
_____
_____
_____
_____

- Go to forgiveness

- Offer reconciliation. Meet to discuss so you can apologize for anything you have done and discuss things openly. Then follow the rest of process. If they refuse, then you can live in forgiveness, in freedom, and always willing to immediately begin the process of reconciliation if and when the other party is ready.

- Continue respect, kindness, and honor whenever we see the other person or are in their presence.

> **Read Luke 10:1-16.**
>
> Jesus Sends Out the Seventy-Two
> **10** After this the Lord appointed seventy-two[a] others and sent them on ahead of him, two by two, into every town and place where he himself was about to go. ² And he said to them, "The harvest is plentiful, but the laborers are few. Therefore pray earnestly to the Lord of the harvest to send out laborers into

LESSON 8:
PRACTICAL WAYS OF RECONCILIATION IN A VARIETY OF SITUATIONS

> his harvest. ³ Go your way; behold, I am sending you out as lambs in the midst of wolves. ⁴ Carry no moneybag, no knapsack, no sandals, and greet no one on the road. ⁵ Whatever house you enter, first say, 'Peace be to this house!' ⁶ And if a son of peace is there, your peace will rest upon him. But if not, it will return to you. ⁷ And remain in the same house, eating and drinking what they provide, for the laborer deserves his wages. Do not go from house to house. ⁸ Whenever you enter a town and they receive you, eat what is set before you. ⁹ Heal the sick in it and say to them, 'The kingdom of God has come near to you.' ¹⁰ But whenever you enter a town and they do not receive you, go into its streets and say, ¹¹ 'Even the dust of your town that clings to our feet we wipe off against you. Nevertheless know this, that the kingdom of God has come near.' ¹² I tell you, it will be more bearable on that day for Sodom than for that town.
>
> Woe to Unrepentant Cities
> ¹³ "Woe to you, Chorazin! Woe to you, Bethsaida! For if the mighty works done in you had been done in Tyre and Sidon, they would have repented long ago, sitting in sackcloth and ashes. ¹⁴ But it will be more bearable in the judgment for Tyre and Sidon than for you. ¹⁵ And you, Capernaum, will you be exalted to heaven? You shall be brought down to Hades.
>
> ¹⁶ "The one who hears you hears me, and the one who rejects you rejects me, and the one who rejects me rejects him who sent me."

Jesus lived in complete forgiveness and offered reconciliation through truth to many. The disciples (in the first part of His ministry, there were over 200 following Him) found His words about eating His flesh and drinking His blood to be too difficult. Their mistake was not being willing to process the confusing truth further and inquiring as to what Jesus actually meant. If they had done so, Jesus would have explained that He didn't mean to eat His physical body and drink His physical blood, but that the life He offered was Himself, that He was the bread of life. But, they didn't inquire any further and just left. Jesus allowed them not to be reconciled and let them leave. In turning to His closest 12 disciples, He asked them if they intended to leave as well. If they answered in the affirmative, He would have allowed them to go, too.

Another example here is the rich young ruler who desired to know the key to eternal life. He acknowledged he had performed all the requirements of the law, but when Jesus asked him to take a step of faith to demonstrate what was actually in his heart, he could not. He became sorrowful and left. Again, Jesus allowed him to not be reconciled and let him go.

LESSON 8:
PRACTICAL WAYS OF RECONCILIATION IN A VARIETY OF SITUATIONS

Both of these case studies show us how we are to act. Christ specifically instructs us to offer peace to others. Out of our own forgiveness, we offer an opportunity to others to receive forgiveness and live in God's Kingdom through His reconciliation based upon truth. We offer this each and every time we offer reconciliation. If the other party is willing to process the hurt and truth, then we are to continue and stay with it until we reach a solution and reconciliation. If they are unwilling to process reconciliation and our peace, then we are to dust our feet off and move on; always remembering to live with the heart of forgiveness and a willingness to reengage within a moment if they come back at a later date and say they are willing to process truth.

In the situation I described with the executive who had rejected an opportunity to sit down and talk through what had happened, I was able to dust off my feet and move forward without being burdened by his actions toward me. Because I was in forgiveness and had "dusted off my feet," when he was willing to come back a year later and process the truth, I eagerly and immediately responded. Being in that position of freedom, (whenever someone who has cut us off from relationship is then willing to get together), our hearts are open and desirous of working toward reconciliation, our calling by God. However, if they remain separated from us (their choice), then we can continue to live in freedom and not be burdened by their unwillingness.

5. What about the person who says they are willing to talk, but are never willing to admit and deal with what they have done to hurt me (denial and rationalization)?

Though they may not be willing to process any truth, our role is to move the level of reconciliation from none to partial. You will need to:

- Be willing to have a surface relationship

- Offer respect, kindness, honor

- Establish healthy boundaries while maintaining honor;

  - Pray for protection of their heart

  - Practice avoiding getting drawn into unhealthy situations and responding when buttons are pushed

  - If limited time, remember this is for a short time and eventually can release it all.

LESSON 8:
PRACTICAL WAYS OF RECONCILIATION IN A VARIETY OF SITUATIONS

Even though they may not be willing to process any truth, our role is still to move the level of reconciliation from a severed relationship to a partial one, as much as it relies upon us. Just as when we were discussing parents, we must be willing to have only a surface relationship while continuing to treat them with respect, kindness, and honor. Remember, establishing healthy boundaries can be accomplished by:

- Praying for the protection of our heart
- Practicing avoidance when it comes to getting drawn into unhealthy situations
- Avoiding response when our "hot buttons" are pushed
- Reminding yourself that it is only for a short time (if there is a time limit) and the release will come when the time is over.

In the situation I described with my mother, we were never able to deal with what she had done to hurt and abuse me in our family. In fact, if I had attempted to push it, it would only have made things worse and served to separate us farther. So, we accepted that we would have only partial reconciliation, where we could not talk much about deep things. In addition, we established appropriate boundaries so that we were not drawn into unhealthy situations for me and my family, all while maintaining the level of reconciliation available to us and not attempting to establish it as an all or nothing relationship.

6. How do I let myself off the hook?

- Forgiveness on the same basis as above
- Reconciliation to God's truth

Read Romans 8:1-2.

Life in the Spirit
8 There is therefore now no condemnation for those who are in Christ Jesus. [a] 2 For the law of the Spirit of life has set you[b] free in Christ Jesus from the law of sin and death.

LESSON 8:
PRACTICAL WAYS OF RECONCILIATION IN A VARIETY OF SITUATIONS

_____
_____
_____
_____
_____

Remember all the truths and benefits listed above, particularly forgetting and redemption.

> **Read Philippians 3:12-16.**
>
> Straining Toward the Goal
> ¹² Not that I have already obtained this or am already perfect, but I press on to make it my own, because Christ Jesus has made me his own. ¹³ Brothers, I do not consider that I have made it my own. But one thing I do: forgetting what lies behind and straining forward to what lies ahead, ¹⁴ I press on toward the goal for the prize of the upward call of God in Christ Jesus. ¹⁵ Let those of us who are mature think this way, and if in anything you think otherwise, God will reveal that also to you. ¹⁶ Only let us hold true to what we have attained.

_____
_____
_____
_____
_____

> **Read Romans 8:38-39 (does not mention past).**
>
> ³⁸ For I am sure that neither death nor life, nor angels nor rulers, nor things present nor things to come, nor powers, ³⁹ nor height nor depth, nor anything else in all creation, will be able to separate us from the love of God in Christ Jesus our Lord.

LESSON 8:
PRACTICAL WAYS OF RECONCILIATION IN A VARIETY OF SITUATIONS

_____
_____
_____
_____
_____

To process truth:

- Is reconciliation needed?

- Is restitution needed?

- Do we need to let go of the past, release, live in truth of God's forgiveness and move on to high calling of Christ Jesus? Yes!

This is perhaps the most interesting and difficult area of forgiveness and reconciliation that encumbers us and keeps us in bondage. Many times, we acknowledge our own mistakes and things done in the past causing us to live in guilt and sorrow and knowing we have caused harm or damage to others. However, much of the time we neglect to acknowledge we have caused harm and damage to ourselves. We are suffering the consequences of our choices, and the consequences are not pleasant. We know we are the cause of our consequences, and because we are fully aware of our own shortcomings and mistakes, we have moved away from God's will for our lives and expect never to be restored again. These lies keep us in sorrow and resignation, as we constantly beat ourselves up over our failures. The remedy regarding our own mistakes is no different than if we were dealing with another person: We must go through the process of forgiveness. We are the ones who have to be reconciled to God's truth. We are the ones who must work through the process of forgiveness and reconciliation until we can let ourselves "off the hook" and be fully released from the past. Again, we must remember God's forgiveness is not based on what we (I, you) deserve but rather on the work Christ has already done in our lives. He has already forgiven us and released us from our past.

All of the truths and benefits listed above still apply to us regarding our own animosity against self. We particularly need to remember how God forgets our sin, and the redemption offered is free and freely given.

We must abide in God's Word until the truth that there is now *no* condemnation in Christ Jesus becomes real to us. Notice that Jesus does not say only that He does not condemn you but that there is no condemnation in Christ Jesus. This

LESSON 8:
PRACTICAL WAYS OF RECONCILIATION IN A VARIETY OF SITUATIONS

means that He is not condemning you or me, no one else is condemning you or me, and neither are we to condemn ourselves! We can and should learn that we can completely release the past and just press forward to what God has in store for you and me. If we can maintain living in this forgiveness and be fully reconciled to Him and the freedom it brings, then we are in a position for God to restore our lives to walk in the beauty of His covenant promises for all who follow Him. We need not live any longer in guilt, for when we do, it is a testimony of how we are not living according to the Spirit, and contrarily to God's very nature. We are called to live in the Kingdom of God: righteousness, peace and joy, freedom, and wonder where He will restore to you and me the exceptional life we either lost or walked away from. It is likely that before we are fully able to forgive others, we truly need to process forgiving ourselves in order to step into God's light and life, receiving His nature which allows us to forgive others each and every time.

We need to process the truth of our relationship to God at all costs. We need reconciliation to God before we can tell others it is possible. We need restoration before others can see the testimony of it in our own lives. We must let go of our past, release it, and choose to live in the truth of God's forgiveness. Then we need to move on, beyond our past, to the high calling of Christ Jesus.

I personally had to work through this most difficult area of forgiveness. As a young executive I was encouraged to increase our family's wealth through real estate investments. While I was managing a division for a Fortune 500 company, I spent a few hours a week developing a commercial real estate project in a different state: I purchased the land, constructed an office building, leased the building, and then sold the building. Along with a few investors, we made an amazing amount of money in a short period of time. I decided I could expand this effort by doing three buildings at once and achieving even more financial gain as a result, particularly since it had been so easy on the first one.

My wife, Linda, completely disagreed and felt that something was wrong. She strongly opposed me moving in this direction. Since she could not explain to me exactly why and I was rather stubborn, I proceeded with making the investments along with some of the other investors' money. This occurred at the beginning of the 1980s when the economy took a big nosedive, and commercial buildings were sitting empty as businesses failed to expand due to the economy. (Remember the Resolution Trust? It was set up by the government to handle all the failed real estate from banks that had loaned money to people who had no wherewithal to cover the shortfalls? I was one of those people.) But the empty building and the interest payments still had to be paid and eventually all of our gain from the prior building, as well as all my personal stock and savings, were depleted with no solution in sight.

LESSON 8:
PRACTICAL WAYS OF RECONCILIATION IN A VARIETY OF SITUATIONS

The banks who owned the loans on the buildings required me to file Chapter 7 bankruptcy and took back the properties, processing the properties through the Resolution Trust. Here I was, a Christian, a seminary graduate, and executive who had just stubbornly ignored God's will and experienced the consequence of that stubbornness—losing all of our family's financial assets.

Though we were able to keep our house, I can still remember the day that the car companies came to pick up our automobiles, and the day I had to purchase back from the bankruptcy court our furniture and my wife's jewelry, including her wedding ring. Needless to say, I was despondent and filled with grief and guilt. One thing that was interesting was that my wife only once said, "I told you so," and forgave me. I was also surprised to learn that it didn't matter to our children. The material things that we owned were really of no interest to them; they just cared about us being together as a family. My daughter, Michelle, who was nine at the time, would write on a whiteboard outside of my bedroom every morning a Scripture verse of hope, followed by her daily signature line, "It will be all right, Daddy." While I could receive their forgiveness, I could not forgive myself or let myself off the hook. I caused this and I deserved what had happened to me. Being encouraged to learn this important issue of forgiving self, every day I would walk with Scriptures about forgiveness and process my heart and feelings with the Lord. Through the daily time processing in the Word, about eight months later it broke for me. God had clearly stated that He had forgiven me and that I had no right to reject this forgiveness in my own life, and toward myself. I was to let go of the past and move on. When it broke and the burden lifted, I again received a life of freedom, moving forward into the beautiful restoration and redemption of God's life for us without care about what had already happened.

I've come to know that God is the God of "now," what has passed is the past, and He encourages us to fully release the past and walk into the fullness of the abundant life that He has planned for us now. This is particularly true since He can restore and create new things from our lousy choices and mistakes. As I have shared on several occasions, this reminds me of a GPS in an automobile. If we go off track, the automobile says make a legal U-turn and get back on track. Often, we think we know better, so we continue on our course, off-track. We eventually wind up so far off the original route, that it isn't beneficial to go back to the point where we went off-track. So, the GPS begins recalculating and establishes a new route to get us to our desired destination. I believe that God is so sovereign that He is fully able to recalculate and reestablish new paths for us to reach the fullness of life ahead of us. He is not limited by our past mistakes and the good news is that restoration is always available to us. His only invitation to us is: "How about now?"

LESSON 8:
PRACTICAL WAYS OF RECONCILIATION IN A VARIETY OF SITUATIONS

I fully received that there is now no condemnation for those who are in Christ Jesus, and thus I no longer needed to live in guilt, but simply repentance, moving on to the high calling of Christ Jesus. We are called to thoroughly enjoy the beautiful relationship offered to us by our Lord Jesus Christ.

7. What about marriage: What is our call to reconcile?

Marriage is the only relationship where we are called to reconcile all the time, every time, 100 percent of the time. We are commanded to live in complete unity.

> **Read Psalm 133.**
>
> When Brothers Dwell in Unity
> A Song of Ascents. Of David.
> **133** Behold, how good and pleasant it is
>   when brothers dwell in unity![a]
> ² It is like the precious oil on the head,
>   running down on the beard,
> on the beard of Aaron,
>   running down on the collar of his robes!
> ³ It is like the dew of Hermon,
>   which falls on the mountains of Zion!
> For there the Lord has commanded the blessing,
>   life forevermore.

_____
_____
_____
_____
_____

LESSON 8:
PRACTICAL WAYS OF RECONCILIATION IN A VARIETY OF SITUATIONS

> **Read Psalm 128.**
>
> Blessed Is Everyone Who Fears the Lord
> A Song of Ascents.
> **128** Blessed is everyone who fears the Lord,
>   who walks in his ways!
> ² You shall eat the fruit of the labor of your hands;
>   you shall be blessed, and it shall be well with you.
> ³ Your wife will be like a fruitful vine
>   within your house;
> your children will be like olive shoots
>   around your table.
> ⁴ Behold, thus shall the man be blessed
>   who fears the Lord.
> ⁵ The Lord bless you from Zion!
>   May you see the prosperity of Jerusalem
>   all the days of your life!
> ⁶ May you see your children's children!
>   Peace be upon Israel!

_____
_____
_____
_____
_____

> **Read Ecclesiastes 9:7-10.**
> **Enjoy Life with the One You Love**
>
> ⁷ Go, eat your bread with joy, and drink your wine with a merry heart, for God has already approved what you do.
>
> ⁸ Let your garments be always white. Let not oil be lacking on your head.

LESSON 8:
PRACTICAL WAYS OF RECONCILIATION IN A VARIETY OF SITUATIONS

> [9] Enjoy life with the wife whom you love, all the days of your vain[a] life that he has given you under the sun, because that is your portion in life and in your toil at which you toil under the sun. [10] Whatever your hand finds to do, do it with your might,[b] for there is no work or thought or knowledge or wisdom in Sheol, to which you are going.

> **Read Ecclesiastes 4:9-12.**
>
> [9] Two are better than one, because they have a good reward for their toil. [10] For if they fall, one will lift up his fellow. But woe to him who is alone when he falls and has not another to lift him up! [11] Again, if two lie together, they keep warm, but how can one keep warm alone? [12] And though a man might prevail against one who is alone, two will withstand him—a threefold cord is not quickly broken.

LESSON 8:
PRACTICAL WAYS OF RECONCILIATION IN A VARIETY OF SITUATIONS

> **Read Philippians 2:1-4.**
> **Christ's Example of Humility**
>
> **2** So if there is any encouragement in Christ, any comfort from love, any participation in the Spirit, any affection and sympathy, ² complete my joy by being of the same mind, having the same love, being in full accord and of one mind. ³ Do nothing from selfish ambition or conceit, but in humility count others more significant than yourselves. ⁴ Let each of you look not only to his own interests, but also to the interests of others.

___
___
___
___
___

> **Read Ephesians 4:1-6.**
> **Unity in the Body of Christ**
>
> **4** I therefore, a prisoner for the Lord, urge you to walk in a manner worthy of the calling to which you have been called, ² with all humility and gentleness, with patience, bearing with one another in love, ³ eager to maintain the unity of the Spirit in the bond of peace. ⁴ There is one body and one Spirit—just as you were called to the one hope that belongs to your call—⁵ one Lord, one faith, one baptism, ⁶ one God and Father of all, who is over all and through all and in all.

___
___
___
___
___

LESSON 8:
PRACTICAL WAYS OF RECONCILIATION IN A VARIETY OF SITUATIONS

The relationship of marriage is built upon God's ordained central relationship, and that is that the two shall become one: to move in and live within unity, complete agreement, and oneness. (Genesis 2:18-25). In contrast to all other relationships where we can allow them to not be reconciled to us if they are unwilling to process truth, we are called to pursue reconciliation with our spouse all the time and every time, regardless of whether they are willing to process truth or not. We are commanded to remain in forgiveness, to ask them to sit down and process truth in a safe and healthy environment, and then work toward a resolution and solution that are truly acceptable to both. In the majority of situations, it is the tenderness paired with humility that will open heart issues and lead the way to true reconciliation. In this way, the marriage can and will be lived out in the exceptional way God intends. We are not called to give up or dust off our feet at any cost, but rather continually work toward full reconciliation. If for some reason, usually due to past unhealthy patterns of your marriage, the other party is not willing to sit down and work through the truth toward reconciliation, then invite them to go to counseling with a third-party believer who can assist the process in opening up wounds and providing techniques allowing for safe communication. However, there are situations where there is a refusal to go to counseling and a refusal to process anything toward reconciliation. In these scenarios it is legitimate to separate for a time (this can be in different rooms in the same house or if severe and highly contentious then perhaps in different locations), but always maintaining a forgiving heart and willingness to process truth—keep asking to work toward resolving the issues in a healthy way and offer your willingness to do anything, including getting third party help to facilitate this. If the other party seeks divorce, we are again called to seek reconciliation with all that is within us, but if they truly desire to file divorce then you are to let them go as long as you have always approached it with a forgiving and tender heart. This should only be a last resort.

As a testimony, my wife and I have been married 50 years. In the beginning years, we struggled with arguing and debating and somewhat considered divorce as a solution though we knew we were called as believers to somehow stay with it. Without fully realizing God's command for marriage, we had a sense that we were to attempt to continue to work at it and learn to reconcile. Until we learned the process of true forgiveness, we were lousy at attempting reconciliation. It was more about negotiation, and since I was a better debater, I could successfully negotiate a win for myself the majority of the time. Though she may have lost the arguments, she got me back in other ways by being passive aggressive, withholding intimacy, spending money, etc. We still were

LESSON 8:
PRACTICAL WAYS OF RECONCILIATION IN A VARIETY OF SITUATIONS

battling and had no real sense of what reconciliation looked like. We existed together but we were not in oneness. After we learned forgiveness, and then understood from Scripture the processes of reconciliation, we were able to come to that complete and whole level of reconciliation. We still have disagreements, we still have moments of anger, and still hurt each other, but because we know that we are called to full reconciliation, we simply follow the process: individual forgiveness toward each other, and then sit down with honor and respect to process the truth until we get a solution. If we do not readily find a solution, we allow ourselves to let it remain as is, continue to enjoy our day, our night, our weekend, and then come back in prayer until God gives us the solution. We choose to remember how simple it is: either He changes my heart, He changes my spouse's heart, or He shows us something new we both did not understand. His solution and His will are best, and there is none better. We always live in full reconciliation. It is pure joy and our marriage continues to get sweeter and sweeter.

www.ingramcontent.com/pod-product-compliance
Lightning Source LLC
Chambersburg PA
CBHW042024100526
44587CB00029B/4290